Contents

Cambridge School Shakespeare

This edition of *The Tempest* is part of the *Cambridge School Shakespeare* series. Like every other play in the series, it has been specially prepared to help all students in schools and colleges.

This *The Tempest* aims to be different from other editions of the play. It invites you to bring the play to life in your classroom, hall or drama studio through enjoyable activities that will increase your understanding. Actors have created their different interpretations of the play over the centuries. Similarly, you are encouraged to make up your own mind about *The Tempest*, rather than having someone else's interpretation handed down to you.

Cambridge School Shakespeare does not offer you a cut-down or simplified version of the play. This is Shakespeare's language, filled with imaginative possibilities. You will find on every left-hand page: a summary of the action, an explanation of unfamiliar words, a choice of activities on Shakespeare's language, characters and stories.

Between each act and in the pages at the end of the play, you will find notes, illustrations and activities. This will help to increase your understanding of the whole play.

There are a large number of activities to give you the widest choice to suit your own particular needs. Please don't think you have to do every one. Choose the activities that will help you most.

This edition will be of value to you whether you are studying for an examination, reading for pleasure, or thinking of putting on the play to entertain others. You can work on the activities on your own or in groups. Many of the activities suggest a particular group size, but don't be afraid to make up larger or smaller groups to suit your own purposes.

Although you are invited to treat *The Tempest* as a play, you don't need special dramatic or theatrical skills to do the activities. By choosing your activities, and by exploring and experimenting, you can make your own interpretations of Shakespeare's language, characters and stories. Whatever you do, remember that Shakespeare wrote his plays to be acted, watched and enjoyed.

Rex Gibson

This edition of *The Tempest* uses the text of the play established by David Lindley in *The New Cambridge Shakespeare.*

CAMBRIDGE SCHOOL

Shakespeare

The Tempest

Series Editor: Rex Gibson
Director, Shakespeare and Schools Project

CAMBRIDGE
UNIVERSITY PRESS

PUBLISHED BY THE PRESS SYNDICATE OF THE UNIVERSITY OF CAMBRIDGE
The Pitt Building, Trumpington Street, Cambridge, United Kingdom

CAMBRIDGE UNIVERSITY PRESS
The Edinburgh Building, Cambridge CB2 2RU, UK
40 West 20th Street, New York, NY 10011–4211, USA
10 Stamford Road, Oakleigh, VIC 3166, Australia
Ruiz de Alarcón 13, 28014 Madrid, Spain
Dock House, The Waterfront, Cape Town 8001, South Africa

http://www.cambridge.org

First published 1995
Sixth printing 2001

Printed in the United Kingdom at the University Press, Cambridge

A catalogue record for this book is available from the British Library

Library of Congress Cataloguing in Publication data applied for

ISBN 0 521 47903 7

Designed by Richard Morris, Stonesfield Design
Picture research by Callie Kendall

Thanks are due to the following for permission to reproduce photographs:

6, 8, 30, 38, 68, 77, 78, 112, 123, 134, 140, 165, Donald Cooper © Photostage; 22, 161, Shakespeare Centre Library, Stratford-upon-Avon; 43, 62, 98, 128, 163, Angus McBean (print by Shakespeare Centre Library, Stratford-upon-Avon); 46, Terence Hoyles; 86, Clive Barda/Performing Arts Library; 103, Gordon Goode/Shakespeare Centre Library, Stratford-upon-Avon; 120, © Abisag Tüllmann, Overlindau 51, 6 Frankfurt/Main, Germany; 157, Mary Evans Picture Library; 159, Michael le Poer Trench; 171, Joe Cocks Studio Collection/Shakespeare Centre Library

List of characters

The island

PROSPERO the rightful Duke of Milan
MIRANDA his daughter
ARIEL an airy spirit
CALIBAN a savage and deformed slave
SPIRITS in Prospero's service

IRIS, CERES, JUNO, NYMPHS, REAPERS — characters in the masque

The shipwrecked royal court

ALONSO King of Naples
FERDINAND Alonso's son
SEBASTIAN Alonso's brother
ANTONIO Prospero's brother, the usurping Duke of Milan
GONZALO an honest old councillor
ADRIAN, FRANCISCO — lords
STEPHANO a drunken butler
TRINCULO a jester

The ship's crew

MASTER the captain
BOATSWAIN
MARINERS

The play takes place on a ship and an island

The Master commands the Boatswain to save the ship from running aground. The Boatswain finds his work hampered by the courtiers. He orders them to go back to their cabins.

1 Staging the tempest (in large groups)

Every director of *The Tempest* faces the problem of how to stage this opening scene. It takes place on a ship at sea during a terrible storm. How can the fury of the waves and wind be shown on stage? In some productions, the scene is played on a bare stage, without props or scenery. The illusion of a ship caught in a tempest is created only by lighting, sounds and the actors' movements. Other productions use an elaborate set to create a realistic ship.

How would you stage Scene I to greatest dramatic effect? Talk together about the following points, then act out the scene. There are six speaking parts, and as many sailors as you wish.

a Explore ways of performing the first stage direction: '*A tempestuous noise of thunder and lightning*'.

b Work out how the actors' movements can suggest a ship caught in a storm.

c How could you convey the sense of fear and crisis? These are people who are desperately concerned to save their lives. Do they panic, or are they well-disciplined?

d What simple props could suggest a ship? One production had only a large ship's wheel at the back of the stage. The sailors struggled to turn it to keep the ship on course.

e Traditional authority is challenged in the storm. The Boatswain is in charge, rather than the higher status passengers. He orders the king and the other aristocrats off the deck. Work out how to show the audience, as clearly as possible, this reversal of traditional social roles.

What cheer? What news?
Good friend
Fall to't yarely get a move on
Bestir quickly
Tend attend, listen
room space to sail in safety
Play the men act like men, command the sailors
keep below stay in your cabins
mar spoil, hinder
roarers wild waves and winds

The Tempest

ACT I SCENE I
A ship at sea

A tempestuous noise of thunder and lightning. Enter a SHIPMASTER, a BOATSWAIN and MARINERS

MASTER Boatswain!

BOATSWAIN Here, master. What cheer?

MASTER Good; speak to th'mariners. Fall to't yarely, or we run ourselves aground. Bestir, bestir! *Exit*

BOATSWAIN Heigh, my hearts! Cheerly, cheerly, my hearts! Yare, yare! Take in the topsail. Tend to th'master's whistle. [*To the storm*] Blow till thou burst thy wind, if room enough!

Enter ALONSO, SEBASTIAN, ANTONIO, FERDINAND, GONZALO *and others*

ALONSO Good boatswain, have care. Where's the master? Play the men.

BOATSWAIN I pray now, keep below.

ANTONIO Where is the master, boatswain?

BOATSWAIN Do you not hear him? You mar our labour – keep your cabins. You do assist the storm.

GONZALO Nay, good, be patient.

BOATSWAIN When the sea is. Hence! What cares these roarers for the name of king? To cabin. Silence! Trouble us not.

GONZALO Good, yet remember whom thou hast aboard.

The Boatswain reminds Gonzalo of Humanity's weakness in the face of Nature's violence. Gonzalo finds comfort in the Boatswain's face. The Boatswain again rebukes the courtiers, and is cursed in return.

1 Challenging authority (in pairs)

The Boatswain is the character with lowest social status in the scene; yet he is clearly in charge. He speaks to his social superiors with little or no respect: 'Out of our way', 'What do you here?', 'Work you then'. He gives his orders to the sailors with confident authority.

a To whom does he speak?
One person reads aloud everything the Boatswain speaks in Scene 1, pausing after each sentence or phrase. In each pause, the other identifies the person the Boatswain is addressing, and his likely tone of voice on each occasion.

b A metaphor for the play?
Both the storm and the Boatswain's behaviour represent the many challenges to authority which will recur throughout the play. As you read on, look out for instances of such disruptions of order.

2 'His complexion is perfect gallows'

Gonzalo's wry comment on the Boatswain's face (line 26) echoes the saying, 'He that is born to be hanged, will never be drowned'. Imagine that the actor playing Gonzalo asks you, 'Is Gonzalo just being cynical, or what? How should I play these lines?' Make your reply.

3 Courteous language? (in pairs)

Sebastian and Antonio curse the Boatswain (lines 36–7, 39–40). Talk together about whether or not you think their bad language is justified, and what it suggests about their characters.

work a peace of the present stop the storm
hand a rope work (handle a rope)
mischance disaster
hap happen
cable anchor
Bring her … main-course use the mainsail
office Captain's whistle
give o'er stop work
warrant him from guarantee him against
unstanched wench talkative or immoral woman

BOATSWAIN None that I more love than myself. You are a councillor; if you can command these elements to silence, and work a peace of the present, we will not hand a rope more – use your authority. If you cannot, give thanks you have lived so long, and make yourself ready in your cabin for the mischance of the hour, if it so hap. [*To the mariners*] Cheerly, good hearts. [*To the courtiers*] Out of our way, I say.

[*Exeunt Boatswain with some of the mariners, followed by Alonso, Sebastian, Antonio, Ferdinand*]

GONZALO I have great comfort from this fellow. Methinks he hath no drowning mark upon him, his complexion is perfect gallows. Stand fast, good Fate, to his hanging; make the rope of his destiny our cable, for our own doth little advantage. If he be not born to be hanged, our case is miserable. *Exit*

Enter BOATSWAIN

BOATSWAIN Down with the topmast! Yare, lower, lower! Bring her to try with main-course.

(*A cry within*)

A plague upon this howling! They are louder than the weather, or our office.

Enter SEBASTIAN, ANTONIO *and* GONZALO

Yet again? What do you here? Shall we give o'er and drown? Have you a mind to sink?

SEBASTIAN A pox o'your throat, you bawling, blasphemous, incharitable dog.

BOATSWAIN Work you then.

ANTONIO Hang, cur, hang, you whoreson, insolent noisemaker, we are less afraid to be drowned than thou art.

GONZALO I'll warrant him from drowning, though the ship were no stronger than a nutshell, and as leaky as an unstanched wench.

The Boatswain orders action to save the ship, but disaster strikes. Antonio again curses the Boatswain. The crew abandon hope. Gonzalo accepts whatever is to come, but wishes for death on land.

'We split, we split!' A Japanese staging of the shipwreck. The passengers and crew face death in different ways. Some sailors pray or beg God's mercy. Others bid farewell to each other or to their wives and children. The Boatswain takes comfort in drink (line 47), and is cursed by Antonio.

1 Shakespeare's invitation

The stage direction '*Enter* MARINERS, *wet*' is Shakespeare's invitation to your imagination. Explore different ways of transforming it into exciting theatrical action!

Lay her a-hold heave-to (furl the sail)
lay her off sail out to sea (the Boatswain changes his order)
wide-chopped big-mouthed
ten tides pirates were condemned to be hanged and to have three tides wash over their bodies
gape at wid'st to glut him open up to swallow him
long heath, brown furze heather, gorse
The wills above God's will
fain rather

BOATSWAIN Lay her a-hold, a-hold; set her two courses. Off to sea again; lay her off!

Enter MARINERS, *wet*

MARINERS All lost! To prayers, to prayers, all lost!

BOATSWAIN What, must our mouths be cold?

GONZALO The king and prince at prayers! Let's assist them,
For our case is as theirs.

SEBASTIAN I'm out of patience.

ANTONIO We're merely cheated of our lives by drunkards.
This wide-chopped rascal – would thou mightst lie drowning
The washing of ten tides!

GONZALO He'll be hanged yet,
Though every drop of water swear against it,
And gape at wid'st to glut him.

[*Exeunt Boatswain and mariners*]

A confused noise within

'Mercy on us!' –
'We split, we split!' – 'Farewell, my wife and children!' –
'Farewell, brother!' – 'We split, we split, we split!'

ANTONIO Let's all sink wi'th'king.

SEBASTIAN Let's take leave of him.

[*Exeunt Sebastian and Antonio*]

GONZALO Now would I give a thousand furlongs of sea for an acre of barren ground – long heath, brown furze, anything. The wills above be done, but I would fain die a dry death. *Exit*

Miranda begs her father, Prospero, to calm the tempest. She feels the suffering of the shipwrecked people, and is full of pity for them. Prospero assures her that no harm has been done.

'There's no harm done.' Prospero assures Miranda that everyone on board the wrecked ship is safe.

1 First sight of Prospero

It is now revealed that the tempest of Scene 1 was caused by Prospero's 'art' (magic). The shipwreck was an illusion, and the passengers and crew are all safe. Some productions begin Scene 2 with Prospero shown very obviously as a powerful magician, his arms raised as he calms the storm at Miranda's request. Other productions begin the scene quietly, after the storm has ended, in contrast to the frenzied activity of Scene 1. Decide how you would stage this first sight of Prospero and Miranda to greatest dramatic effect.

art magic
allay calm
pitch tar
welkin's cheek sky's face
brave noble, fine
or ere before
fraughting souls passengers
Be collected be calm
piteous pitying
full poor cell humble cave
meddle with enter, mingle with

Act 1 Scene 2
The island

Enter PROSPERO and MIRANDA

MIRANDA If by your art, my dearest father, you have
Put the wild waters in this roar, allay them.
The sky it seems would pour down stinking pitch,
But that the sea, mounting to th'welkin's cheek,
Dashes the fire out. O I have suffered
With those that I saw suffer! A brave vessel,
Who had no doubt some noble creature in her,
Dashed all to pieces. O the cry did knock
Against my very heart! Poor souls, they perished.
Had I been any god of power, I would
Have sunk the sea within the earth, or ere
It should the good ship so have swallowed, and
The fraughting souls within her.

PROSPERO Be collected;
No more amazement. Tell your piteous heart
There's no harm done.

MIRANDA O, woe the day.

PROSPERO No harm.
I have done nothing but in care of thee –
Of thee my dear one, thee my daughter – who
Art ignorant of what thou art, nought knowing
Of whence I am, nor that I am more better
Than Prospero, master of a full poor cell,
And thy no greater father.

MIRANDA More to know
Did never meddle with my thoughts.

Prospero decides to tell Miranda her life story. He again assures her that no one was hurt in the shipwreck, and questions her about what she remembers. He reveals that he was once Duke of Milan.

---

1 Prospero's 'magic garment'

Prospero wears a 'magic garment' which gives him the supernatural powers that he calls his 'art'. In stage productions, the 'magic garment' is usually a cloak, richly decorated with magical symbols (see page 165).

Design your own version of Prospero's 'magic garment'.

2 Father and daughter (in pairs)

Prospero is about to tell Miranda how she came to the island. To gain a first impression of Prospero's story, take parts and read lines 25–186.

Experiment with different ways of speaking Prospero's lines. For example, is his style gentle and loving, or pompous and authoritarian? Or ...?

3 'In the dark backward and abysm of time'

Close your eyes, repeat line 50 to yourself several times, and try to conjure up an image in your mind of Prospero's words ('abysm' means abyss, or bottomless gulf). Is your image sharp or blurred? Try to focus on different parts of it. Think of possible reasons why Shakespeare chose these particular words, rather than saying 'long ago'.

---

direful spectacle terrible sight
very virtue essence
provision foresight
soul person
perdition loss
Betid happened
bootless inquisition unsuccessful enquiry
an assurance a certainty
warrants guarantees
tended waited on
dark backward and abysm dim depths
aught ere anything before

PROSPERO 'Tis time
I should inform thee farther. Lend thy hand
And pluck my magic garment from me – so –
[*Miranda assists Prospero; his cloak is laid aside*]
Lie there my art. Wipe thou thine eyes; have comfort.
The direful spectacle of the wrack which touched
The very virtue of compassion in thee,
I have with such provision in mine art
So safely ordered, that there is no soul,
No, not so much perdition as an hair
Betid to any creature in the vessel
Which thou heard'st cry, which thou saw'st sink. Sit down,
For thou must now know farther.
[*Miranda sits*]

MIRANDA You have often
Begun to tell me what I am, but stopped
And left me to a bootless inquisition,
Concluding, 'Stay: not yet.'

PROSPERO The hour's now come;
The very minute bids thee ope thine ear,
Obey, and be attentive. Canst thou remember
A time before we came unto this cell?
I do not think thou canst, for then thou wast not
Out three years old.

MIRANDA Certainly, sir, I can.

PROSPERO By what? By any other house, or person?
Of any thing the image, tell me, that
Hath kept with thy remembrance.

MIRANDA 'Tis far off;
And rather like a dream than an assurance
That my remembrance warrants. Had I not
Four or five women once, that tended me?

PROSPERO Thou hadst, and more, Miranda. But how is't
That this lives in thy mind? What seest thou else
In the dark backward and abysm of time?
If thou rememb'rest aught ere thou cam'st here,
How thou cam'st here thou mayst.

MIRANDA But that I do not.

PROSPERO Twelve year since, Miranda, twelve year since,
Thy father was the Duke of Milan and
A prince of power –

Prospero again confirms that he was once the Duke of Milan. As Prospero wanted to pursue his studies, he made his brother, Antonio, ruler of the state. But the treacherous Antonio seized all power from Prospero.

---

1 'A prince of power'

Prospero describes how he was once the unchallenged ruler of the most important state in Italy: 'Through all the signories (Italian states) it was the first, / And Prospero the prime duke'. But because of his over-whelming interest in acquiring magical skills ('secret studies'), Prospero entrusted the government of Milan to Antonio, his brother.

Antonio proved to be false. To serve his own interests, he learned who to promote, and who to cut down to size ('Who t'advance, and who To trash for over-topping'). He won the loyalty of Prospero's followers ('new created…new formed 'em'). Antonio now had both the people and the position ('officer, and office') to make everyone in Milan dance to his tune. Like a parasitic ivy which destroys the tree it grows on, he took over all of Prospero's powers.

Here's how an actor who played Prospero described lines 66–87:

> This is the first time Prospero has told Miranda what happened. He's choked with the passion and pain of remembering. So, his thoughts and words are disjointed and compressed, and his story wanders, especially when he recalls how all-important he used to be. Some of his anger spills over on to Miranda when he thinks she's not listening!

Speak the lines several times. Then decide:

- whether you think Prospero is 'choked with passion and pain'.
- whether you think 'his thoughts and words are disjointed and compressed'.
- whether you think he becomes angry with Miranda.

---

piece of virtue model of faithfulness
no worse issued similarly noble
heaved thence thrown out of Milan
holp hither helped here
o'th'teen of the trouble
is from my remembrance I've forgotten
perfidious treacherous
put…my state gave rule over my dukedom
transported / And rapt in enchanted by
grant suits bestow favours
verdure sap, life

MIRANDA Sir, are not you my father?
PROSPERO Thy mother was a piece of virtue, and
She said thou wast my daughter; and thy father
Was Duke of Milan; and his only heir,
And princess, no worse issued.
MIRANDA O the heavens!
What foul play had we, that we came from thence?
Or blessèd was't we did?
PROSPERO Both, both, my girl.
By foul play, as thou say'st, were we heaved thence,
But blessedly holp hither.
MIRANDA O my heart bleeds
To think o'th'teen that I have turned you to,
Which is from my remembrance. Please you, farther.
PROSPERO My brother and thy uncle, called Antonio –
I pray thee mark me, that a brother should
Be so perfidious – he, whom next thyself
Of all the world I loved, and to him put
The manage of my state, as at that time
Through all the signories it was the first,
And Prospero the prime duke, being so reputed
In dignity, and for the liberal arts
Without a parallel; those being all my study,
The government I cast upon my brother,
And to my state grew stranger, being transported
And rapt in secret studies. Thy false uncle –
Dost thou attend me? –
MIRANDA Sir, most heedfully.
PROSPERO Being once pèrfected how to grant suits,
How to deny them; who t'advance, and who
To trash for over-topping; new created
The creatures that were mine, I say, or changed 'em,
Or else new formed 'em; having both the key
Of officer, and office, set all hearts i'th'state
To what tune pleased his ear, that now he was
The ivy which had hid my princely trunk,
And sucked my verdure out on't – thou attend'st not!
MIRANDA O good sir, I do.

Prospero describes how his neglect of his duties aroused his brother's evil nature. Enjoying the benefits of playing the duke, Antonio aspired to become the duke, and plotted with Alonso, the King of Naples.

1 'Awaked an evil nature'

Prospero passionately recalls his brother's treachery. Lines 88–116 show his state of mind:

a I neglected the business of government ('worldly ends').

b I sought privacy ('closeness') in order to study.

c But what I studied was beyond the citizens' interest or understanding.

d My retirement was the cause of my brother's evil acts.

e My absolute trust in him was completely betrayed.

f He abused my wealth and over-taxed my people.

g He came to believe his own lies that he was the duke.

h Therefore his ambition grew.

i He wished to become the part he played – the duke.

j I was content with my books. He saw this as my showing that I was unfit to govern.

k Eager for power, he agreed to make Milan subordinate to the King of Naples.

Match **a–k** above with the appropriate lines, then read on to discover what happens next, as Antonio seizes power in Milan.

---

beget bring out
sans bound without limit
thus lorded so like a duke
revènue wealth
into truth invented reality
prerogative authority
Absolute Milan the real duke
temporal royalties worldly power
confederates makes a treaty with
So dry he was for sway so eager for power
tribute protection money
condition treaty terms

PROSPERO I pray thee mark me:
I, thus neglecting worldly ends, all dedicated
To closeness, and the bettering of my mind
With that which, but by being so retired,
O'er-prized all popular rate, in my false brother
Awaked an evil nature; and my trust,
Like a good parent, did beget of him
A falsehood, in its contrary as great
As my trust was – which had indeed no limit,
A confidence sans bound. He being thus lorded,
Not only with what my revènue yielded,
But what my power might else exact – like one
Who having into truth by telling of it,
Made such a sinner of his memory
To credit his own lie – he did believe
He was indeed the duke, out o'th'substitution
And executing th'outward face of royalty
With all prerogative. Hence his ambition growing –
Dost thou hear?
MIRANDA Your tale, sir, would cure deafness.
PROSPERO To have no screen between this part he played,
And him he played it for, he needs will be
Absolute Milan. Me, poor man, my library
Was dukedom large enough. Of temporal royalties
He thinks me now incapable; confederates –
So dry he was for sway – wi'th'King of Naples
To give him annual tribute, do him homage,
Subject his coronet to his crown, and bend
The dukedom yet unbowed – alas, poor Milan –
To most ignoble stooping.
MIRANDA O the heavens!
PROSPERO Mark his condition, and th'event, then tell me
If this might be a brother.
MIRANDA I should sin
To think but nobly of my grandmother –
Good wombs have borne bad sons.

Alonso made a treaty with Antonio to overthrow Prospero. Antonio treacherously admitted Alonso's army into Milan. Prospero and Miranda were captured and cast adrift in a tiny, unseaworthy boat.

---

1 The overthrow of Prospero (in small groups)

Prospero's story continues. His old enemy, Alonso, King of Naples, agreed a treaty ('condition') with Antonio. The agreement was that, in exchange for ('in lieu o'th'premises') making Milan subordinate to Naples, *and* for protection money ('tribute'), Alonso would overthrow Prospero and make Antonio Duke of Milan. Under cover of darkness, the treacherous Antonio opened the city gates to give Alonso's accomplices ('ministers') the opportunity to capture Prospero and Miranda. The conspirators dared not kill Prospero because of his popularity. Instead, they abandoned him and his infant daughter in a tiny, unseaworthy boat ('a rotten carcass of a butt').

The opposite page is only part of Prospero's story of his usurpation (overthrow of a rightful ruler), but it has great potential for drama and stage business. Experiment with ways of speaking Prospero's lines. For example, you could read them very quickly, the words tumbling out passionately as Prospero remembers with anger. Alternatively, you could read them very slowly and reflectively as if the experience was like recalling a long-ago dream.

2 Mime the action (in small groups)

Prepare a slow motion mime to convey Prospero's words. One person slowly speaks Prospero's lines 120–32 and 140–51, pausing at the end of each small unit of meaning. In the pause, the others mime the actions described.

---

inveterate of long standing
hearkens…suit listened to Antonio's proposal
presently extirpate immediately expel (or destroy)
levied gathered
Fated destined
hint occasion, event
impertinent irrelevant
durst not dared not
In few briefly
barque ship
leagues sea miles

PROSPERO Now the condition.
This King of Naples, being an enemy
To me inveterate, hearkens my brother's suit,
Which was, that he, in lieu o'th'premises
Of homage, and I know not how much tribute,
Should presently extirpate me and mine
Out of the dukedom, and confer fair Milan,
With all the honours, on my brother. Whereon,
A treacherous army levied, one midnight
Fated to th'purpose did Antonio open
The gates of Milan, and i'th'dead of darkness
The ministers for th'purpose hurried thence
Me, and thy crying self.

MIRANDA Alack, for pity!
I, not remembering how I cried out then,
Will cry it o'er again; it is a hint
That wrings mine eyes to't.

PROSPERO Hear a little further,
And then I'll bring thee to the present business
Which now's upon's; without the which, this story
Were most impertinent.

MIRANDA Wherefore did they not
That hour destroy us?

PROSPERO Well demanded, wench;
My tale provokes that question. Dear, they durst not,
So dear the love my people bore me; nor set
A mark so bloody on the business; but
With colours fairer painted their foul ends.
In few, they hurried us aboard a barque,
Bore us some leagues to sea, where they prepared
A rotten carcass of a butt, not rigged,
Nor tackle, sail, nor mast – the very rats
Instinctively have quit it. There they hoist us
To cry to th'sea, that roared to us; to sigh
To th'winds, whose pity sighing back again
Did us but loving wrong.

MIRANDA Alack, what trouble
Was I then to you!

Prospero says that he found comfort and strength in Miranda's smile, in divine providence and in Gonzalo's help. Fortune now favours him, his enemies are within his reach. He causes Miranda to fall asleep.

---

1 Three kinds of help

In lines 152–68, Prospero tells of the three things which sustained him in all his troubles:

lines 153–8 Miranda's smile 'raised in me / An undergoing stomach' (made me determined to survive)
line 159 'providence divine' (the help of the gods)
lines 160–8 Gonzalo's practical help.

Write notes for the actor playing Prospero to help him make the three kinds of help even clearer to the audience. For example, he could gently touch Miranda's smiling face at 'which' in line 156.

2 'Knowing I loved my books…'

Gonzalo had made sure that books were placed in the boat which carried Prospero unwillingly to exile. But what were these volumes that Prospero valued above his dukedom?

Invent titles for four or five books which you think would be appropriate to Prospero's 'secret studies' (see also page 159).

3 'Now I arise' (in pairs)

The stage direction at line 169 shows that Prospero is speaking quite literally (I now stand up). But the line could also have a symbolic meaning (my fortunes are improving), which is directly implied in line 179, when Prospero calls Fortune 'my dear lady' (fortune is now on my side). She has delivered his enemies into his hands.

Talk together about whether or not you think Shakespeare intended both a literal and symbolic meaning in line 169.

---

cherubin young angel
Infusèd with a fortitude full of endurance
decked covered, ornamented
stuffs materials
steaded much greatly helped us
profit benefit
prescience foreknowledge, insight
zenith highest point of fortune
auspicious favourable
court befriend, use
omit neglect

PROSPERO [*Sitting*] O, a cherubin
Thou wast that did preserve me. Thou didst smile,
Infusèd with a fortitude from heaven,
When I have decked the sea with drops full salt,
Under my burden groaned; which raised in me
An undergoing stomach, to bear up
Against what should ensue.
MIRANDA How came we ashore?
PROSPERO By providence divine.
Some food we had, and some fresh water, that
A noble Neapolitan, Gonzalo,
Out of his charity – who being then appointed
Master of this design – did give us, with
Rich garments, linens, stuffs, and necessaries
Which since have steaded much. So, of his gentleness,
Knowing I loved my books, he furnished me
From mine own library, with volumes that
I prize above my dukedom.
MIRANDA Would I might
But ever see that man.
PROSPERO [*Standing*] Now I arise.
Sit still, and hear the last of our sea-sorrow.
Here in this island we arrived, and here
Have I, thy schoolmaster, made thee more profit
Than other princes can, that have more time
For vainer hours, and tutors not so careful.
MIRANDA Heavens thank you for't. And now I pray you, sir –
For still 'tis beating in my mind – your reason
For raising this sea-storm?
PROSPERO Know thus far forth:
By accident most strange, bountiful Fortune,
Now my dear lady, hath mine enemies
Brought to this shore; and by my prescience
I find my zenith doth depend upon
A most auspicious star, whose influence
If now I court not, but omit, my fortunes
Will ever after droop. Here cease more questions.
Thou art inclined to sleep. 'Tis a good dullness,
And give it way; I know thou canst not choose.

Prospero calls Ariel, who reports that he has carried out Prospero's commands in exact detail. Ariel's miraculous display of fire caused terror on the ship. Ferdinand was the first passenger to leap overboard.

---

1 Enact Ariel's story

Lines 187–215 offer many possibilities for acting out.

a Whole class
Each person in the group learns a very short section of Ariel's lines. There can be twenty to thirty 'units'. One person plays Prospero, and stands in the centre of the room. In order, each 'Ariel' runs to join Prospero, speaking 'his' words, and making appropriate accompanying gestures.

b In pairs
Repeat it! One person speaks a short section, the other echoes it. Try different styles of echoing, such as whispering, questioning, emphatically, slowly, rapidly.

c On your own
Walk around the room reading Ariel's lines aloud. Change direction abruptly at every punctuation mark. Add suitable gestures.

2 St Elmo's fire

Ariel's description of how he 'flamed amazement' all over the ship is like the strange effect of light called St Elmo's fire, well-known to sailors caught in storms at sea. Shakespeare's imagination may have been stirred by a letter written by William Strachey in 1610, which told of such fantastic lightning seen during a shipwreck off Bermuda (see pages 152–3).

---

grave sir most wise master
task command
all his quality all his fellow spirits
to point in exact detail
beak prow
in the waist amidships
yards yard-arm
precursors forerunners
Neptune king of the sea
coil turmoil, confusion
tricks of desperation despairing actions
nigh shore near land

[*Miranda sleeps; Prospero puts on his magic robe*]
Come away, servant, come; I'm ready now.
Approach, my Ariel. Come!

Enter ARIEL

ARIEL All hail, great master, grave sir, hail! I come
To answer thy best pleasure; be't to fly,
To swim, to dive into the fire, to ride
On the curled clouds. To thy strong bidding task
Ariel, and all his quality.
PROSPERO Hast thou, spirit, performed to point the tempest
That I bade thee?
ARIEL To every article.
I boarded the king's ship. Now on the beak,
Now in the waist, the deck, in every cabin,
I flamed amazement. Sometime I'd divide
And burn in many places; on the topmast,
The yards and bowsprit, would I flame distinctly,
Then meet and join. Jove's lightning, the precursors
O'th'dreadful thunder-claps, more momentary
And sight-outrunning were not; the fire and cracks
Of sulphurous roaring the most mighty Neptune
Seem to besiege, and make his bold waves tremble,
Yea, his dread trident shake.
PROSPERO My brave spirit!
Who was so firm, so constant, that this coil
Would not infect his reason?
ARIEL Not a soul
But felt a fever of the mad, and played
Some tricks of desperation. All but mariners
Plunged in the foaming brine and quit the vessel,
Then all a-fire with me; the king's son Ferdinand,
With hair up-staring – then like reeds, not hair –
Was the first man that leaped; cried 'Hell is empty,
And all the devils are here.'
PROSPERO Why that's my spirit.
But was not this nigh shore?
ARIEL Close by, my master.
PROSPERO But are they, Ariel, safe?

Ariel reports that the ship's passengers are safe on shore, the sailors are asleep on board, and the rest of the fleet is returning to Naples, mourning Alonso. Ariel demands his freedom.

1 Resentful servants

In traditional tales, the spirits who serve magicians are often resentful. Magicians are never completely in control. Prospero and Ariel seem to be no exception to that tradition. But how does Ariel make his demand for freedom: with open resentment, or with controlled politeness, or…? Advise the actor playing Ariel how to deliver lines 242–50.

sustaining buoyant (supporting in the sea)
troops groups
odd angle remote corner
deep nook secret bay
still-vexed always stormy
charm spell
mid season noon
two glasses two o'clock
most preciously without waste
the time be out the proper time
prithee pray you
bate me let me off

ARIEL Not a hair perished;
On their sustaining garments not a blemish,
But fresher than before. And as thou bad'st me,
In troops I have dispersed them 'bout the isle.
The king's son have I landed by himself,
Whom I left cooling of the air with sighs
In an odd angle of the isle, and sitting,
His arms in this sad knot.
PROSPERO Of the king's ship,
The mariners, say how thou hast disposed,
And all the rest o'th'fleet?
ARIEL Safely in harbour
Is the king's ship, in the deep nook, where once
Thou call'dst me up at midnight to fetch dew
From the still-vexed Bermudas, there she's hid;
The mariners all under hatches stowed,
Who, with a charm joined to their suffered labour,
I've left asleep. And for the rest o'th'fleet –
Which I dispersed – they all have met again,
And are upon the Mediterranean float
Bound sadly home for Naples,
Supposing that they saw the king's ship wracked,
And his great person perish.
PROSPERO Ariel, thy charge
Exactly is performed; but there's more work.
What is the time o'th'day?
ARIEL Past the mid season.
PROSPERO At least two glasses. The time 'twixt six and now
Must by us both be spent most preciously.
ARIEL Is there more toil? Since thou dost give me pains,
Let me remember thee what thou hast promised,
Which is not yet performed me.
PROSPERO How now? Moody?
What is't thou canst demand?
ARIEL My liberty.
PROSPERO Before the time be out? No more.
ARIEL I prithee,
Remember I have done thee worthy service,
Told thee no lies, made no mistakings, served
Without or grudge or grumblings. Thou did promise
To bate me a full year.

Prospero rebukes Ariel, accusing him of resentfulness. Prospero reminds Ariel of Sycorax who, enraged by Ariel's refusal to obey her, imprisoned him inside a tree for twelve years.

---

1 Ariel's appearance

Ariel is Prospero's servant. His past errands have taken him to the ocean floor, to the freezing north wind, and to rivers running deep underground (lines 252–6). Turn to the pictures of Ariel on pages 22, 62, 98 and 161. Which comes closest to your image of an Ariel who could perform such amazing feats?

2 'The foul witch Sycorax' (in small groups)

No one really knows why Shakespeare decided to use the name Sycorax for the witch who tormented Ariel. Some people think that the name may come from two Greek words: *sys* (sow) and *korax* (raven). But whatever Sycorax's name means, Prospero's tale offers wonderful opportunities for using your imagination.

Work together on lines 257–67 to produce a dramatic presentation of the first part of Sycorax's story. Your enactment could be a mime or short play, but it should show clearly:

Sycorax's appearance 'with age and envy / was grown into a hoop'.
'mischiefs manifold' What were her many mischievous acts?
'sorceries terrible to enter human hearing' for example?

There was 'one thing she did' which caused the people of Algiers to spare her life. What was it? Let your imaginations run!

You will find further activities on the story of Sycorax and Ariel on page 26.

---

think'st it much resent having
do me business work for me
with child pregnant
abhorred hateful
grand hests terrible commands
potent ministers powerful spirits
unmitigable uncalmable, unquenchable
cloven split
rift cleft
litter give birth to
whelp dog

PROSPERO Dost thou forget
From what a torment I did free thee?
ARIEL No.
PROSPERO Thou dost! And think'st it much to tread the ooze
Of the salt deep,
To run upon the sharp wind of the north,
To do me business in the veins o'th'earth
When it is baked with frost.
ARIEL I do not, sir.
PROSPERO Thou liest, malignant thing. Hast thou forgot
The foul witch Sycorax, who with age and envy
Was grown into a hoop? Hast thou forgot her?
ARIEL No, sir.
PROSPERO Thou hast. Where was she born? Speak. Tell me.
ARIEL Sir, in Algiers.
PROSPERO O, was she so? I must
Once in a month recount what thou hast been,
Which thou forget'st. This damned witch Sycorax,
For mischiefs manifold, and sorceries terrible
To enter human hearing, from Algiers
Thou know'st was banished. For one thing she did
They would not take her life. Is not this true?
ARIEL Ay, sir.
PROSPERO This blue-eyed hag was hither brought with child,
And here was left by th'sailors. Thou, my slave,
As thou report'st thyself, was then her servant;
And for thou wast a spirit too delicate
To act her earthy and abhorred commands,
Refusing her grand hests, she did confine thee,
By help of her more potent ministers,
And in her most unmitigable rage,
Into a cloven pine, within which rift
Imprisoned thou didst painfully remain
A dozen years; within which space she died,
And left thee there; where thou didst vent thy groans
As fast as mill-wheels strike. Then was this island –
Save for the son that she did litter here,
A freckled whelp, hag-born – not honoured with
A human shape.
ARIEL Yes, Caliban her son.

Prospero describes how he released Ariel, but threatens further punishment if Ariel continues to complain. He orders Ariel to disguise himself as an invisible sea-nymph, wakes Miranda and proposes to visit Caliban.

---

1 Imprisonment and release (whole class)

Lines 269–93 vividly tell the story of Ariel and Sycorax. Experiment with ways of acting out the story, showing each section of the script as imaginatively as possible. For example, one person acts as narrator, pausing after each short section. In the pause, the others mime the action. Alternatively, divide the class into three groups. Each group prepares and acts out the following sections, using a mixture of Shakespeare's language and your own:

Group 1 lines 269–77 ('This blue-eyed hag…cloven pine')
Group 2 lines 277–81 ('within which rift…mill-wheels strike')
Group 3 lines 286–93 ('Thou best know'st…and let thee out')

To help your preparation talk together about each of the following:

- What were Sycorax's 'earthy and abhorred commands' and her 'grand hests' which Ariel refused to carry out?
- How might you show a 'cloven pine' (a split pine tree)?
- How can you show an '*unmitigable* rage' (unable to be calmed)?
- How might you show 'mill-wheels strike' (the blades of a water-wheel hitting the water)?
- How did the 'ever-angry bears' show their pity?
- What did Prospero do to release Ariel (what was his 'art')?

2 Master and servant

Prospero threatens Ariel with a further twelve years' imprisonment, this time wedged into an oak tree! Suggest how Prospero and Ariel could speak lines 293–9. For example, does Ariel ask for pardon humbly and sincerely, or resentfully and moodily?

---

penetrate the breasts evoke pity
rend split
correspondent obedient
diligence care
Heaviness drowsiness
miss do without
serves in offices does duties

PROSPERO Dull thing, I say so: he, that Caliban
Whom now I keep in service. Thou best know'st
What torment I did find thee in. Thy groans
Did make wolves howl, and penetrate the breasts
Of ever-angry bears. It was a torment
To lay upon the damned, which Sycorax
Could not again undo. It was mine art,
When I arrived and heard thee, that made gape
The pine, and let thee out.

ARIEL I thank thee, master.

PROSPERO If thou more murmur'st, I will rend an oak
And peg thee in his knotty entrails till
Thou hast howled away twelve winters.

ARIEL Pardon, master.
I will be correspondent to command
And do my spiriting gently.

PROSPERO Do so;
And after two days I will discharge thee.

ARIEL That's my noble master! What shall I do?
Say what? What shall I do?

PROSPERO Go make thyself
Like to a nymph o'th'sea. Be subject to
No sight but thine and mine, invisible
To every eye-ball else. Go take this shape
And hither come in't. Go! Hence with diligence.
Exit [Ariel]

PROSPERO [*To Miranda*] Awake, dear heart, awake; thou hast slept well,
Awake.

MIRANDA The strangeness of your story put
Heaviness in me.

PROSPERO Shake it off. Come on,
We'll visit Caliban, my slave, who never
Yields us kind answer.

MIRANDA 'Tis a villain, sir,
I do not love to look on.

PROSPERO But as 'tis
We cannot miss him. He does make our fire,
Fetch in our wood, and serves in offices
That profit us. What ho! Slave! Caliban!
Thou earth, thou! Speak!

Ariel is given secret orders by Prospero. Caliban curses Prospero and Miranda. Prospero threatens painful punishments. Caliban recalls how Prospero had treated him kindly at first, but then enslaved him.

---

1 **Learning to curse** (in pairs)

Prospero and Caliban threaten and curse each other vehemently. Collect up all the threats and curses from lines 314–74. Take parts and hurl them at each other, one by one. Afterwards, talk together about the way in which Prospero and Caliban speak to each other. For example, does either of them ever utter a kind word?

2 **'This island's mine'** (in groups of three)

Who has the right to own the island? Many people believe that Caliban's experience is a typical example of what happens to any race subjected to colonisation. Prospero came to the island and made Caliban his slave (see pages 154–7).

Explore the story which unfolds in lines 332–62 from the point of view of either Caliban or Prospero. Take parts and act out the various elements of the story. Alternatively, invent and act out your own version of what happened.

You could consider the following possible interpretations:

a Was Caliban an innocent, naturally good person, whose genuine friendship towards Miranda was misinterpreted? Or was he a savage brute, tamed by Prospero, but whose true nature came out when he tried to rape Miranda?

b Was Prospero a sincere, kind person who had no intention of seizing the island until Caliban's evil nature was revealed? Or was he deceitful and greedy, determined from the outset to exploit the island's natural resources, and always intending to become its sole master, making Caliban his slave?

Fine apparition! well disguised
quaint clever, elegant
got fathered
dam mother
raven bird of ill-omen
fen marsh, bog
south-west unhealthy wind
urchins hedgehogs, goblins
vast of night long stretch of night
bigger light…less sun and moon
brine-pits salt pits
charms spells
sty me imprison me like a pig

CALIBAN (*Within*) There's wood enough within.
PROSPERO Come forth, I say; there's other business for thee.
Come, thou tortoise, when?

Enter ARIEL *like a water-nymph*

Fine apparition! My quaint Ariel,
Hark in thine ear.
[*Whispers to Ariel*]
ARIEL My lord, it shall be done. *Exit*
PROSPERO Thou poisonous slave, got by the devil himself
Upon thy wicked dam, come forth.

Enter CALIBAN

CALIBAN As wicked dew as e'er my mother brushed
With raven's feather from unwholesome fen
Drop on you both! A south-west blow on ye,
And blister you all o'er!
PROSPERO For this, be sure, tonight thou shalt have cramps,
Side-stitches that shall pen thy breath up; urchins
Shall, for that vast of night that they may work,
All exercise on thee; thou shalt be pinched
As thick as honeycomb, each pinch more stinging
Than bees that made 'em.
CALIBAN I must eat my dinner.
This island's mine by Sycorax my mother,
Which thou tak'st from me. When thou cam'st first
Thou strok'st me and made much of me; wouldst give me
Water with berries in't, and teach me how
To name the bigger light, and how the less,
That burn by day and night. And then I loved thee
And showed thee all the qualities o'th'isle,
The fresh springs, brine-pits, barren place and fertile –
Cursèd be I that did so! All the charms
Of Sycorax – toads, beetles, bats – light on you!
For I am all the subjects that you have,
Which first was mine own king; and here you sty me
In this hard rock, whiles you do keep from me
The rest o'th'island.

Prospero accuses Caliban of attempting to rape Miranda. Miranda tells Caliban that he deserves to be imprisoned because he is evil. Caliban curses her but, fearful of Prospero's threats, obeys the order to leave.

'Hag-seed, hence!' Prospero threatens Caliban. (Notice that 'Caliban' is almost an anagram of 'cannibal'.)

1 Miranda or Prospero?

In the first edition of the play, lines 351–62 are spoken by Miranda (as they are in this edition). But for over two hundred years, in both stage productions and printed editions, these lines were given to Prospero. Many people felt that such harsh words were out of character for Miranda. Even today, the lines are sometimes spoken by Prospero. Decide whether or not you would transfer the lines to Prospero, giving reasons for your choice.

stripes lashes
violate / The honour of rape
Abhorrèd hateful, frightful
print imprint, impression
capable of all ill naturally evil
abide bear, endure
red plague bubonic plague
Hag-seed son of a witch
rack torture
Setebos a Patagonian god
vassal slave

PROSPERO Thou most lying slave,
Whom stripes may move, not kindness! I have used thee,
Filth as thou art, with humane care, and lodged thee
In mine own cell, till thou didst seek to violate
The honour of my child.

CALIBAN O ho, O ho! Would't had been done.
Thou didst prevent me – I had peopled else
This isle with Calibans.

MIRANDA Abhorrèd slave,
Which any print of goodness wilt not take,
Being capable of all ill! I pitied thee,
Took pains to make thee speak, taught thee each hour
One thing or other. When thou didst not, savage,
Know thine own meaning, but wouldst gabble like
A thing most brutish, I endowed thy purposes
With words that made them known. But thy vile race –
Though thou didst learn – had that in't which good natures
Could not abide to be with; therefore wast thou
Deservedly confined into this rock,
Who hadst deserved more than a prison.

CALIBAN You taught me language, and my profit on't
Is, I know how to curse. The red plague rid you
For learning me your language!

PROSPERO Hag-seed, hence!
Fetch us in fuel; and be quick, thou'rt best,
To answer other business. Shrug'st thou, malice?
If thou neglect'st, or dost unwillingly
What I command, I'll rack thee with old cramps,
Fill all thy bones with aches, make thee roar,
That beasts shall tremble at thy din.

CALIBAN No, pray thee.
[*Aside*] I must obey; his art is of such power,
It would control my dam's god Setebos,
And make a vassal of him.

PROSPERO So, slave, hence.

Exit Caliban

Ariel's first song is an invitation to dance upon the sands. Ferdinand is amazed by the music which has calmed the storm and his grief. Ariel's second song describes a wonderful transformation after death.

1 'ARIEL *invisible, playing and singing*'

Shakespeare's company probably used a cloak, described in a list of stage properties as 'a robe for to go invisible' to conceal Ariel. But how could Ariel's invisibility be conveyed to an audience today? Make your suggestions.

2 Ariel's songs (in small groups)

Ariel's first song is about the calming of the tempest. It is an invitation to dance by the seashore where the waves kiss, becoming silent and calm ('kissed, / The wild waves whist'). Ariel invites spirits to join in with the chorus of watch-dogs barking and cockerels crowing. Ferdinand says that the music calms both the storm and his feeling of grief for his father (line 390), whom he believes drowned.

Ariel's second song seems to be directly addressed to Ferdinand, to comfort him. It tells how Alonso is magically transformed: his bones into coral, his eyes into pearl. The song reassures the grieving son, telling him to think of his father not as dead, but as having undergone 'a sea-change / Into something rich and strange'.

Explore different ways of singing or speaking the songs. Music is always a vital part of the atmosphere in any Shakespeare play. It deepens meaning and adds to the mood of the scene. Think about what kind of mood you would want to create here. For example, would it be one of harmony and wonder, or something else?

3 First sight of Ferdinand

Write down a few words to describe Ferdinand's appearance. For example, is he bedraggled or refreshed? amazed or confused?

whist into silence
Foot it featly dance daintily
the burden bear sing the chorus
dispersedly separately, not in unison
strain of strutting Chanticleer crowing of a proud cockerel
waits attends
Allaying calming
passion grief
knell funeral bell

Enter FERDINAND, *and* ARIEL *invisible, playing and singing*

SONG

ARIEL Come unto these yellow sands,
And then take hands.
Curtsied when you have, and kissed,
The wild waves whist.
Foot it featly here and there,
And sweet sprites the burden bear.
Hark, hark
The watch-dogs bark
Bow wow, bow wow.
[*Spirits dispersedly echo the burden 'Bow wow'*]
Hark, hark! I hear
The strain of strutting Chanticleer,
Cry cock-a-diddle-dow.
[*Spirits dispersedly echo the burden 'Cock a diddle dow'*]

FERDINAND Where should this music be? I'th'air, or th'earth?
It sounds no more; and sure it waits upon
Some god o'th'island. Sitting on a bank,
Weeping again the king my father's wrack,
This music crept by me upon the waters,
Allaying both their fury and my passion
With its sweet air. Thence I have followed it –
Or it hath drawn me rather; but 'tis gone.
No, it begins again.

SONG

ARIEL Full fathom five thy father lies,
Of his bones are coral made;
Those are pearls that were his eyes;
Nothing of him that doth fade,
But doth suffer a sea-change
Into something rich and strange.
Sea-nymphs hourly ring his knell.
Hark, now I hear them, 'ding dong bell'.
[*Spirits echo the burden 'ding dong bell'*]

Miranda wonders at Ferdinand, imagining him to be a spirit. Prospero assures her that Ferdinand is human. Ferdinand thinks that Miranda is a goddess, and is surprised to hear her speak his language.

1 Elaborate language – a clue to staging?

Prospero's line 407 ('The fringèd curtains of thine eye advance') is a formal and elaborate way of saying 'open your eyes'. Prospero uses another elaborate image in lines 413–14 ('stained / With grief' meaning 'weeping'). Such formal language may be an indication that what follows is to be seen as equally artificial, namely the idea of two people falling in love at first sight. Shakespeare may be reminding you not to view the scene as something from real life. (You will find an activity on page 40 on what implications this has for staging the scene.)

2 'It goes on, I see'

Prospero's plan ('It') is working. Make a guess as to why he wants Miranda and Ferdinand to fall in love.

3 Speaking to a stranger (in pairs)

Decide, giving your reasons, which of these two views best expresses your own ideas about the first meeting of Ferdinand and Miranda:

a 'This is a delicate moment. It is full of dream-like wonder, and a sense of something beyond what is human. Ferdinand believes that Miranda is a goddess. He almost guesses her name ('O you wonder!'), and is amazed to hear her speak his language.'

b 'Ferdinand is a European prince, and he thinks that he is meeting a foreigner who doesn't speak his language. So, he speaks lines 421–6 slowly and emphatically, as if Miranda were stupid.'

---

ditty song
remember recall, commemorate
mortal human
owes owns
brave form handsome appearance
gallant young gentleman
these airs this music
Vouchsafe grant
remain live
bear me behave
the best the most noble (Ferdinand believes he is now King of Naples)

FERDINAND The ditty does remember my drownèd father.
This is no mortal business, nor no sound
That the earth owes. I hear it now above me.
PROSPERO [*To Miranda*] The fringèd curtains of thine eye advance,
And say what thou seest yond.
MIRANDA What is't? A spirit?
Lord, how it looks about! Believe me, sir,
It carries a brave form. But 'tis a spirit.
PROSPERO No, wench, it eats, and sleeps, and hath such senses
As we have, such. This gallant which thou seest
Was in the wrack; and but he's something stained
With grief – that's beauty's canker – thou might'st call him
A goodly person. He hath lost his fellows,
And strays about to find 'em.
MIRANDA I might call him
A thing divine, for nothing natural
I ever saw so noble.
PROSPERO [*Aside*] It goes on, I see,
As my soul prompts it. [*To Ariel*] Spirit, fine spirit, I'll free thee
Within two days for this.
FERDINAND [*Seeing Miranda*] Most sure the goddess
On whom these airs attend. Vouchsafe my prayer
May know if you remain upon this island,
And that you will some good instruction give
How I may bear me here. My prime request,
Which I do last pronounce, is – O you wonder –
If you be maid, or no?
MIRANDA No wonder, sir,
But certainly a maid.
FERDINAND My language? Heavens!
I am the best of them that speak this speech,
Were I but where 'tis spoken.

Ferdinand, believing his father dead, says he is King of Naples. Miranda and Ferdinand have fallen in love. To test their love, Prospero accuses Ferdinand of usurpation. Miranda defends Ferdinand.

---

1 Antonio's son? Miranda's forgetfulness?

The script opposite features two of the many puzzles which occur during *The Tempest*. Lines 436–7 suggest that Antonio ('the Duke of Milan') has a son, but no such person appears in the play. In line 443, Miranda appears to have totally forgotten her father's story about the part the King of Naples played in his overthrow. (You will find an activity on such puzzles on page 82.)

2 Getting a word in

Ferdinand has fallen head over heels in love with Miranda at first sight. He is so entranced by her that Prospero finds it difficult to gain his attention, asking for a 'word' at lines 441, 442, 448 and 451. Prospero seems exasperated at line 451, 'I charge thee / That thou attend me!'.

Advise Ferdinand how to behave in lines 420–58 to show that he only has eyes and ears for Miranda.

3 Beauty = goodness? (in small groups)

Can you tell whether someone is morally good from their appearance? Miranda thinks so. In lines 456–8, she says that Ferdinand's good looks reflect his good character. Good drives out evil from beautiful people ('Good things will strive to dwell with't'). But in *Macbeth*, King Duncan denies this belief: 'there's no art to find the mind's construction in the face'.

Talk together about whether or not you believe a person's character shows in their face. What does Miranda's claim suggest about her own character?

---

single solitary, weak
Myself am Naples I am king
ne'er since at ebb always weeping
twain two
control contradict
I sighed for I loved
your affection not gone forth not in love with someone else
uneasy difficult
light (line 450) easy
light (line 451) cheap
usurp illegally seize
ow'st not do not own

PROSPERO How the best?
What wert thou if the King of Naples heard thee?
FERDINAND A single thing, as I am now, that wonders
To hear thee speak of Naples. He does hear me,
And that he does, I weep. Myself am Naples,
Who, with mine eyes, ne'er since at ebb, beheld
The king my father wracked.
MIRANDA Alack, for mercy!
FERDINAND Yes, faith, and all his lords, the Duke of Milan
And his brave son being twain.
PROSPERO [*Aside*] The Duke of Milan
And his more braver daughter could control thee
If now 'twere fit to do't. At the first sight
They have changed eyes. [*To Ariel*] Delicate Ariel,
I'll set thee free for this! [*To Ferdinand*] A word, good sir;
I fear you have done yourself some wrong; a word.
MIRANDA [*Aside*] Why speaks my father so ungently? This
Is the third man that e'er I saw; the first
That e'er I sighed for. Pity move my father
To be inclined my way.
FERDINAND O, if a virgin,
And your affection not gone forth, I'll make you
The Queen of Naples.
PROSPERO Soft, sir, one word more.
[*Aside*] They are both in either's powers; but this swift business
I must uneasy make, lest too light winning
Make the prize light. [*To Ferdinand*] One word more. I charge thee
That thou attend me! Thou dost here usurp
The name thou ow'st not, and hast put thyself
Upon this island as a spy, to win it
From me, the lord on't.
FERDINAND No, as I am a man.
MIRANDA There's nothing ill can dwell in such a temple.
If the ill spirit have so fair a house,
Good things will strive to dwell with't.

Prospero threatens harsh punishment on Ferdinand, who draws his sword. Prospero 'freezes' Ferdinand with a spell, and forces him to drop the sword. Prospero scolds Miranda for supporting Ferdinand.

'He draws, and is charmed from moving.' Prospero casts a spell on Ferdinand, making him unable to move.

1 'My foot my tutor!'

Prospero's rebuke to Miranda is a vivid way of saying 'shall something inferior presume to teach me?' Does Prospero speak impatiently and angrily, or with amused irony, or in some other tone?

manacle chain
fresh-brook mussels horrible-tasting shellfish
entertainment treatment
too rash a trial too strong a test
gentle of high social status
Come from thy ward stop this sword-play
stick staff
surety guarantee
chide scold
advocate for supporter of
impostor liar, fraud

PROSPERO [*To Ferdinand*] Follow me.
[*To Miranda*] Speak not you for him: he's a traitor. [*To Ferdinand*] Come!
I'll manacle thy neck and feet together;
Sea water shalt thou drink; thy food shall be
The fresh-brook mussels, withered roots, and husks
Wherein the acorn cradled. Follow.

FERDINAND No!
I will resist such entertainment, till
Mine enemy has more power.

He draws, and is charmed from moving

MIRANDA O dear father,
Make not too rash a trial of him, for
He's gentle, and not fearful.

PROSPERO [*To Miranda*] What, I say,
My foot my tutor? [*To Ferdinand*] Put thy sword up, traitor,
Who mak'st a show, but dar'st not strike, thy conscience
Is so possessed with guilt. Come from thy ward,
For I can here disarm thee with this stick,
And make thy weapon drop.

MIRANDA [*Kneeling*] Beseech you, father!

PROSPERO Hence! Hang not on my garments.

MIRANDA Sir, have pity;
I'll be his surety.

PROSPERO Silence! One word more
Shall make me chide thee, if not hate thee. What,
An advocate for an impostor? Hush!
Thou think'st there is no more such shapes as he,
Having seen but him and Caliban. Foolish wench,
To th'most of men this is a Caliban,
And they to him are angels.

MIRANDA My affections
Are then most humble. I have no ambition
To see a goodlier man.

Ferdinand says that, in spite of all his troubles, he will be content if he is allowed to see Miranda once a day from his prison. Prospero promises Ariel freedom in return for his services.

1 Fairy-tale elements (in pairs)

The episode of Ferdinand echoes two major elements of the fairy-tale tradition (the 'romance' stories which probably influenced Shakespeare as he wrote *The Tempest*). Firstly, the harsh father who submits the young lover to trials and ordeals in order to test his love. Secondly, the power of love to overcome all suffering.

a The trials of love

Ferdinand's words give Prospero secret delight because his plan is succeeding ('It works' means Ferdinand and Miranda have fallen in love'). But Prospero plans to submit Ferdinand to harsh treatment to test the strength of his love.

b The power of love

Ferdinand says that the chance to see Miranda once a day outweighs all the adversities which plague him: his father's death, his weakness, the shipwreck, Prospero's threats. The confines of his prison will be space enough for him if he can glimpse Miranda daily. Ferdinand's words strongly suggest the make-believe world of fairy-tale, in which love conquers all. The mere sight of a beloved woman is sufficient to overcome all ills.

Talk together about how you would stage the whole Ferdinand episode (lines 375–500). Would you want to play it to emphasise the unreality and fairy-tale elements? Or would you wish to stage it as naturalistically as possible, as if it were real life?

nerves muscles
in their infancy as weak as a baby
light of little importance
It works my plan is succeeding
unwonted unusual

PROSPERO [*To Ferdinand*] Come on, obey.
Thy nerves are in their infancy again
And have no vigour in them.
FERDINAND So they are.
My spirits, as in a dream, are all bound up.
My father's loss, the weakness which I feel,
The wrack of all my friends, or this man's threats,
To whom I am subdued, are but light to me,
Might I but through my prison once a day
Behold this maid. All corners else o'th'earth
Let liberty make use of; space enough
Have I in such a prison.
PROSPERO [*Aside*] It works. [*To Ferdinand*] Come on!
[*To Ariel*] Thou hast done well, fine Ariel. [*To Ferdinand*] Follow me.
[*To Ariel*] Hark what thou else shalt do me.
MIRANDA [*To Ferdinand*] Be of comfort;
My father's of a better nature, sir,
Than he appears by speech. This is unwonted
Which now came from him.
PROSPERO [*To Ariel*] Thou shalt be as free
As mountain winds; but then exactly do
All points of my command.
ARIEL To th'syllable.
PROSPERO [*To Ferdinand*] Come follow. [*To Miranda*] Speak not for him.

Exeunt

Looking back at Act 1

Activities for groups or individuals

1 Who's in charge?

Act 1 is full of challenges to authority. The Boatswain orders the king and courtiers to leave the deck; Prospero recounts his overthrow by his brother, Antonio; Ariel and Caliban question Prospero's right to keep them as servants; and Prospero accuses Ferdinand of wanting to seize the island from him.

Find quotations in the script to illustrate each of these challenges. Talk together about each one, trying to decide whether or not the questioning of authority is justified. Which of them could truthfully be called an act of usurpation (the overthrow by force of a rightful ruler)?

2 Telling stories

In Scene 2, Prospero tells the story of how Antonio stole his dukedom (lines 66–168), and of Ariel's imprisonment by Sycorax (lines 257–93). Ariel describes how he brought about the shipwreck (lines 195–215). Caliban's story explains how he welcomed Prospero, but was condemned to slavery (lines 332–45).

Choose one of these stories and prepare a dramatic presentation of it, perhaps using a narrator to describe the events as they happen.

3 Different views of Prospero

Freeze into five different 'statues' of Prospero to show how he is seen differently by Miranda, Ariel, Caliban, Ferdinand and Antonio. Show one of your 'frozen pictures' to other students, and ask them to guess which character's view it portrays. Then think about your own view of Prospero from the evidence in Act 1. As you read on, see if you want to revise your view.

4 Prospero's overthrow

Neither television nor newspapers existed in Shakespeare's time. But imagine that they did! Show how *The Milan Times* or *Televisione Milano* reported the news of Prospero's overthrow and banishment by his brother, Antonio. Remember that Antonio may have seized control of the media to ensure that his story is the only one that is heard.

Compare this 1951 staging of the shipwreck with the illustration of the same scene on page 6. Think about how you could explain the differences between the two stagings.

5 Clash of cultures?

In Scene 2, lines 351–62, Miranda claims that Caliban's true nature is resistant to goodness ('Which any print of goodness will not take', meaning 'it is impossible to stamp or impress morality into his nature'). She says that Caliban comes from a 'vile race' which is hateful to 'good natures'. Talk together about your views on whether Miranda's own words are full of hatred because they assume the inferiority of other cultures (see also pages 154–7).

When one country colonises or conquers another, it often imposes its own language on the defeated people. Like Miranda, the conquering nation describes the native language as 'gabble', and assumes that it has no meaning. But do you think that Miranda is right when she says that Caliban could not express himself? Or do you think it more likely that she did not understand his language?

Gonzalo tries to cheer Alonso up by reminding him of their miraculous survival. Sebastian mocks Gonzalo, deliberately mistaking his words. Alonso begs Gonzalo to be quiet.

---

1 Two groups of courtiers (in groups of six)

King Alonso is in deep grief, mourning Ferdinand whom he believes drowned. His courtiers form two very distinct groups. Gonzalo, Adrian and Francisco will comfort the king. They seek to find good in what has happened to them. In sharp contrast, Sebastian and Antonio are cynical and mocking. They joke together, especially at Gonzalo's expense.

To gain a first impression of the two groups of courtiers, take parts as Alonso and the five courtiers, and read lines 1–177. Sit or stand in separate groups as you read, in order to emphasise the differences between the courtiers' characters (see also the illustration on page 77).

2 Puns

Sebastian and Antonio continually play with language in the first half of this scene. Audiences in Shakespeare's day particularly enjoyed this kind of witty word-play, although some of the puns are obscure today. Explaining the humour can kill the joke, but here's some help with the puns on the opposite page:

lines 9–11 'peace', 'porridge' (porridge was made of peas)
line 17 'entertainer' (Gonzalo means 'person', Antonio means 'innkeeper')
lines 18–19 'dollar' (money), 'dolour' (sadness).

It's best to read through quickly, making it clear that Antonio and Sebastian are mocking the others. If you stop and try to explain every joke, it becomes tedious. If you read with the styles of the different characters in your mind (mocking versus sincerity), the sense and the humour come through clearly.

Beseech you I beg you
much beyond far greater than
hint cause, occasion
masters of some merchant…merchant owners of a merchant ship and the traders
The visitor the comforter of the sick
give him o'er so give up on him
One: tell it's struck one: keep count
spendthrift waster, chatterbox
I prithee, spare please be quiet

ACT 2 SCENE 1
A remote part of the island

Enter ALONSO, SEBASTIAN, ANTONIO, GONZALO, ADRIAN, FRANCISCO and others

GONZALO Beseech you, sir, be merry. You have cause –
So have we all – of joy; for our escape
Is much beyond our loss. Our hint of woe
Is common; every day some sailor's wife,
The masters of some merchant, and the merchant
Have just our theme of woe. But for the miracle –
I mean our preservation – few in millions
Can speak like us. Then wisely, good sir, weigh
Our sorrow with our comfort.

ALONSO Prithee, peace.

SEBASTIAN [*Apart to Antonio*] He receives comfort like cold porridge.

ANTONIO [*Apart to Sebastian*] The visitor will not give him o'er so.

SEBASTIAN Look, he's winding up the watch of his wit,
By and by it will strike.

GONZALO [*To Alonso*] Sir, –

SEBASTIAN One: tell.

GONZALO When every grief is entertained
That's offered, comes to the entertainer –

SEBASTIAN A dollar.

GONZALO Dolour comes to him indeed; you have spoken truer than you purposed.

SEBASTIAN You have taken it wiselier than I meant you should.

GONZALO Therefore, my lord –

ANTONIO Fie, what a spendthrift is he of his tongue.

ALONSO I prithee, spare.

Antonio and Sebastian mockingly bet on which courtier will speak first. They comment cynically on the optimistic remarks of the others. Gonzalo is amazed that everyone's clothes are clean and dry.

Cynical commentators. Antonio and Sebastian see rottenness and corruption where Gonzalo and Adrian see good (lines 45–55).

crow talk
A match! it's a bet!
desert uninhabited
subtle gentle (Sebastian interprets it as 'crafty')
temperance climate (but Antonio puns on the girl's name)
fen marsh, bog
tawny brown, sunburnt
vouched rarities proclaimed wonders
notwithstanding in spite of that, nevertheless
glosses smart appearance

GONZALO Well, I have done. But yet –

SEBASTIAN He will be talking.

ANTONIO Which, of he or Adrian, for a good wager, first begins to crow?

SEBASTIAN The old cock.

ANTONIO The cockerel.

SEBASTIAN Done. The wager?

ANTONIO A laughter.

SEBASTIAN A match!

ADRIAN Though this island seem to be desert –

ANTONIO Ha, ha, ha!

SEBASTIAN So: you're paid.

ADRIAN Uninhabitable, and almost inaccessible –

SEBASTIAN Yet –

ADRIAN Yet –

ANTONIO He could not miss't.

ADRIAN It must needs be of subtle, tender, and delicate temperance.

ANTONIO Temperance was a delicate wench.

SEBASTIAN Ay, and a subtle, as he most learnedly delivered.

ADRIAN The air breathes upon us here most sweetly.

SEBASTIAN As if it had lungs, and rotten ones.

ANTONIO Or as 'twere perfumed by a fen.

GONZALO Here is everything advantageous to life.

ANTONIO True, save means to live.

SEBASTIAN Of that there's none, or little.

GONZALO How lush and lusty the grass looks! How green!

ANTONIO The ground indeed is tawny.

SEBASTIAN With an eye of green in't.

ANTONIO He misses not much.

SEBASTIAN No, he doth but mistake the truth totally.

GONZALO But the rarity of it is, which is indeed almost beyond credit –

SEBASTIAN As many vouched rarities are.

GONZALO That our garments being, as they were, drenched in the sea, hold notwithstanding their freshness and glosses, being rather new-dyed than stained with salt water.

ANTONIO If but one of his pockets could speak, would it not say he lies?

SEBASTIAN Ay, or very falsely pocket up his report.

Gonzalo continues to marvel at everyone's dry clothes. Antonio and Sebastian laugh sarcastically about Gonzalo's references to widow Dido and to the location of Carthage.

---

1 Widow Dido of Carthage

Gonzalo's lines 65–7 reveal that the court party was returning home from a wedding when the tempest struck. Alonso's daughter, Claribel, has married the King of Tunis.

a 'Widow Dido'

Dido, Queen of Carthage, was a famous figure in Roman mythology. In one version of the myth, she was faithful to her dead husband. But in another version, recounted in Virgil's *Aeneid*, she had a passionate affair with Aeneas, the Trojan Prince who founded Rome. When she was later abandoned by Aeneas, she killed herself.

Antonio and Sebastian's mockery may, therefore, lie in their amazement at hearing the tragic queen, who killed herself for love, described as 'Widow Dido'. It seems an incongruous description, so they comment sarcastically on what they see as Gonzalo's lack of sophistication.

b 'The miraculous harp'

Carthage is close to Tunis. Today (and in Shakespeare's time), the Roman city lies in ruins. Antonio and Sebastian compare Gonzalo to the legendary Amphian, King of Thebes, who raised the city walls by playing his harp. Since Gonzalo mistakes Tunis for Carthage, Sebastian says Gonzalo has built the whole city out of words (line 83).

How could you make the 'widow Dido' lines amusing and meaningful for a modern audience? One production had Antonio and Sebastian emphatically rhyming 'widow' and 'Dido'.

Afric Africa
paragon model of excellence
kernels seeds, pips
Bate except, leave out
doublet short jacket
in a sort in a way, relatively

GONZALO Methinks our garments are now as fresh as when we put them on first in Afric, at the marriage of the king's fair daughter Claribel to the King of Tunis.

SEBASTIAN 'Twas a sweet marriage, and we prosper well in our return.

ADRIAN Tunis was never graced before with such a paragon to their queen.

GONZALO Not since widow Dido's time.

ANTONIO Widow? A pox o'that! How came that widow in? Widow Dido!

SEBASTIAN What if he had said 'widower Aeneas' too? Good Lord, how you take it!

ADRIAN Widow Dido, said you? You make me study of that. She was of Carthage, not of Tunis.

GONZALO This Tunis, sir, was Carthage.

ADRIAN Carthage?

GONZALO I assure you, Carthage.

ANTONIO His word is more than the miraculous harp.

SEBASTIAN He hath raised the wall, and houses too.

ANTONIO What impossible matter will he make easy next?

SEBASTIAN I think he will carry this island home in his pocket, and give it his son for an apple.

ANTONIO And sowing the kernels of it in the sea, bring forth more islands.

GONZALO Ay.

ANTONIO Why, in good time.

GONZALO [*To Alonso*] Sir, we were talking, that our garments seem now as fresh as when we were at Tunis at the marriage of your daughter, who is now queen.

ANTONIO And the rarest that e'er came there.

SEBASTIAN Bate, I beseech you, widow Dido.

ANTONIO O widow Dido? Ay, widow Dido.

GONZALO Is not, sir, my doublet as fresh as the first day I wore it – I mean, in a sort –

ANTONIO That sort was well fished for.

GONZALO – when I wore it at your daughter's marriage?

Alonso refuses to be comforted. He fears that his daughter and son are lost forever. Francisco claims that Ferdinand probably survived. Sebastian blames Alonso for all the disasters, but is reprimanded by Gonzalo.

1 Francisco: a very minor character?

Lines 108–17 (and three words in Act 3 Scene 3, line 40), are Francisco's only words in the play. His description of Ferdinand swimming strongly is full of active verbs ('beat', 'ride', 'trod', 'flung', 'breasted', 'oared'). He paints an image of the cliff bending over, as if to help Ferdinand (lines 115–16).

Imagine that you are directing the play. The actor playing Francisco says to you, 'Please help me. This is my only chance. I've got to make a striking impression on the audience, so I must really exaggerate everything I can in the speech.' What do you reply?

2 Sebastian's malice

In lines 118–30, Sebastian strongly criticises Alonso. With barely concealed racism, Sebastian claims that all the courtiers begged Alonso not to permit the marriage of Claribel to the King of Tunis. Sebastian also asserts that Claribel did not want to marry the African king, but, as a dutiful daughter, she obeyed her father's will. Alonso would not listen to either his courtiers or his daughter, with disastrous results.

Identify one or two words or phrases in each of Sebastian's lines which he could emphasise to hurt Alonso's feelings as much as possible.

---

in my rate in my opinion
surges waves
surge most swol'n huge waves
contentious challenging
his wave-worn basis the foot of the cliff
kneeled to and importuned begged
loathness unwillingness, hatred
beam scale, balance
time to speak it in occasion
chirurgeonly like a surgeon

ALONSO You cram these words into mine ears, against
The stomach of my sense: would I had never
Married my daughter there. For coming thence
My son is lost, and, in my rate, she too,
Who is so far from Italy removed
I ne'er again shall see her. O thou mine heir
Of Naples and of Milan, what strange fish
Hath made his meal on thee?
FRANCISCO Sir, he may live.
I saw him beat the surges under him,
And ride upon their backs; he trod the water
Whose enmity he flung aside, and breasted
The surge most swol'n that met him. His bold head
'Bove the contentious waves he kept, and oared
Himself with his good arms in lusty stroke
To th'shore, that o'er his wave-worn basis bowed,
As stooping to relieve him. I not doubt
He came alive to land.
ALONSO No, no, he's gone.
SEBASTIAN Sir, you may thank yourself for this great loss,
That would not bless our Europe with your daughter,
But rather lose her to an African,
Where she, at least, is banished from your eye,
Who hath cause to wet the grief on't.
ALONSO Prithee, peace.
SEBASTIAN You were kneeled to and importuned otherwise
By all of us; and the fair soul herself
Weighed between loathness and obedience, at
Which end o'th'beam should bow. We have lost your son,
I fear for ever. Milan and Naples have
More widows in them of this business' making
Than we bring men to comfort them. The fault's
Your own.
ALONSO So is the dearest of the loss.
GONZALO My lord Sebastian,
The truth you speak doth lack some gentleness,
And time to speak it in; you rub the sore,
When you should bring the plaster.
SEBASTIAN Very well.
ANTONIO And most chirurgeonly.

Gonzalo seeks to cheer the king with an account of an ideal world, where everything is owned in common. Antonio and Sebastian mock Gonzalo. He criticises their empty sense of humour.

1 Shakespeare's reading

Gonzalo's picture of a society in which ownership of everything is shared ('commonwealth') is heavily influenced by an essay entitled 'On Cannibals', written by a French philosopher, Michel de Montaigne (1533–92). Montaigne argued that the 'savage' societies being discovered in the New World (America) were superior to the sophisticated civilisations of Europe. The essay gave rise to the belief in 'the noble savage', for whom harmonious, peaceful and equal relationships were completely natural. A brief extract from a contemporary translation of Montaigne's essay is given below. Pick out all the words or themes which are echoed in the script opposite:

> It is a nation…that hath no kind of traffic, no knowledge of letters, no intelligence of numbers, no name of magistrate nor of politic superiority, no use of service, of riches or poverty, no contracts, no successions, no dividences, no occupation but idle, no respect of Kindred but common, no apparel but natural, no manuring of lands, no use of wine, corn or metal. The very words that import lying, falsehood, treasons, envy, dissimulation; covetousness, detraction, and pardon were never heard.

2 The ideal society (in small groups)

People have always dreamed about 'Utopia' or 'the golden age'. In these 'ideal' societies, men and women would live together in natural harmony, without the need for governments or armies.

Consider, in turn, each item in Gonzalo's commonwealth: no 'traffic' (commerce, trade); no judges; no 'Letters' (education), and so on. Talk together about whether or not you think each item is both desirable (a 'good' thing), and necessary in any society.

---

plantation colonisation
nettle-seed, docks, mallows weeds
contraries opposite to usual custom
Execute organise
use of service slavery, servants
contract, succession inheritance
Bourn, bound of land, tilth boundaries, fences, agriculture
engine weapon
foison plenty
minister occasion give opportunity
sensible and nimble sensitive and quick (mocking)

GONZALO [*To Alonso*] It is foul weather in us all, good sir,
When you are cloudy.
SEBASTIAN Foul weather?
ANTONIO Very foul.
GONZALO Had I plantation of this isle, my lord –
ANTONIO He'd sow't with nettle-seed.
SEBASTIAN Or docks, or mallows.
GONZALO – And were the king on't, what would I do?
SEBASTIAN 'Scape being drunk, for want of wine.
GONZALO I'th'commonwealth I would by contraries
Execute all things. For no kind of traffic
Would I admit; no name of magistrate;
Letters should not be known; riches, poverty,
And use of service, none; contract, succession,
Bourn, bound of land, tilth, vineyard, none;
No use of metal, corn, or wine, or oil;
No occupation, all men idle, all;
And women too, but innocent and pure;
No sovereignty –
SEBASTIAN Yet he would be king on't.
ANTONIO The latter end of his commonwealth forgets the beginning.
GONZALO All things in common nature should produce
Without sweat or endeavour. Treason, felony,
Sword, pike, knife, gun, or need of any engine
Would I not have; but nature should bring forth
Of it own kind, all foison, all abundance
To feed my innocent people.
SEBASTIAN No marrying 'mong his subjects?
ANTONIO None, man, all idle; whores and knaves.
GONZALO I would with such perfection govern, sir,
T'excel the Golden Age.
SEBASTIAN 'Save his majesty!
ANTONIO Long live Gonzalo!
GONZALO And – do you mark me, sir?
ALONSO Prithee, no more; thou dost talk nothing to me.
GONZALO I do well believe your highness, and did it to minister occasion to these gentlemen, who are of such sensible and nimble lungs, that they always use to laugh at nothing.
ANTONIO 'Twas you we laughed at.

Gonzalo continues to reprimand Antonio and Sebastian. Ariel's music sends some of the courtiers to sleep. Antonio offers to guard Alonso as he sleeps, then hints that Sebastian could become king.

---

1 Gonzalo – irritated or amused? (in pairs)

Gonzalo turns on Antonio and Sebastian, and rebukes them for their mockery. Does he show genuine anger, or does he scold them in an amused, ironic tone?

Experiment with ways of speaking everything Gonzalo says in lines 167–81 to decide on an appropriate style.

2 Contemporary echoes

Shakespeare's audience would be aware of the implications of certain references which today require explanation:

line 163 ''Save his majesty'. A Jacobean law forbade oaths which used God's name (as in 'God save...').

lines 175–7 'you would lift the moon out of her sphere...changing'. Gonzalo says that the two courtiers would steal the moon from its orbit if only it stayed still long enough. He also echoes the contemporary proverb 'the moon still shines in spite of all the barking of dogs'.

line 178 'go a-batfowling'. Birds were caught by attracting them with a light and striking them with bats (sticks). Sebastian says that he and Antonio would use the stolen moon as such a light (to catch fools).

3 Antonio – peace-maker or mocker?

How do you think Antonio should speak his lines 179 and 182? Is he still taunting Gonzalo, or is he trying to make peace?

---

flat-long harmlessly (flat side of a sword)
sphere orbit
a-batfowling catching birds
warrant guarantee
adventure my discretion risk my reputation
heavy sleepy
nimble wide awake
Th'occasion speaks thee this is your opportunity

GONZALO Who, in this kind of merry fooling, am nothing to you; so you may continue, and laugh at nothing still.
ANTONIO What a blow was there given!
SEBASTIAN And it had not fall'n flat-long.
GONZALO You are gentlemen of brave mettle; you would lift the moon out of her sphere, if she would continue in it five weeks without changing.

Enter ARIEL [*invisible*] *playing solemn music*

SEBASTIAN We would so, and then go a-batfowling.
ANTONIO Nay, good my lord, be not angry.
GONZALO No, I warrant you, I will not adventure my discretion so weakly. Will you laugh me asleep, for I am very heavy?
ANTONIO Go sleep, and hear us.
[*All sleep except Alonso, Sebastian and Antonio*]
ALONSO What, all so soon asleep? I wish mine eyes
Would with themselves shut up my thoughts; I find
They are inclined to do so.
SEBASTIAN Please you, sir,
Do not omit the heavy offer of it.
It seldom visits sorrow; when it doth,
It is a comforter.
ANTONIO We two, my lord,
Will guard your person while you take your rest,
And watch your safety.
ALONSO Thank you. Wondrous heavy.
[*Alonso sleeps. Exit Ariel*]
SEBASTIAN What a strange drowsiness possesses them?
ANTONIO It is the quality o'th'climate.
SEBASTIAN Why
Doth it not then our eyelids sink? I find
Not myself disposed to sleep.
ANTONIO Nor I; my spirits are nimble.
They fell together all, as by consent
They dropped, as by a thunder-stroke. What might,
Worthy Sebastian, O, what might? – No more.
And yet, methinks I see it in thy face,
What thou shouldst be. Th'occasion speaks thee, and
My strong imagination sees a crown
Dropping upon thy head.

Sebastian is puzzled by Antonio's words, but comes to see significance in them. He asks Antonio for advice. Antonio says that fear and idleness cause failure, and asserts confidently that Ferdinand has drowned.

1 Temptation (in pairs)

Having already seized the throne of his brother Prospero, Antonio begins to encourage Sebastian to do likewise, and usurp Alonso's throne. This 'temptation' episode has been compared to the way in which Lady Macbeth spurs Macbeth on to the murder of Duncan (see *Macbeth*, Act 1 Scene 5, lines 52–71 and Act 1 Scene 7, lines 29–82). It also has echoes in *King John* in which the king prompts Hubert to murder Arthur.

To gain a first impression of how the two plotters work out their murderous plan, take parts and read lines 191–289. Put your heads as close together as possible, and whisper the lines to each other. As you speak, think about how the lines could be spoken on stage. For example:

- Are there long pauses as Sebastian slowly realises that Antonio is prompting him to murder his own brother?
- Do they sit or stand face to face and make eye contact, or does Antonio deliberately avoid meeting Sebastian's gaze, except at particular moments?
- How quickly does Sebastian realise what Antonio has in mind?

2 An apt image

Sebastian says he is like 'standing water' (line 213), when the tide is about to turn and neither withdraws (ebbs) nor goes forward (flows). His own inclination is to ebb, to go backwards. Antonio responds that Sebastian's joking comparison is much more powerful than he suspects. It implies that people who are fearful or idle will not succeed in life.

---

wink'st shut your eyes
if heed me if you take my advice
Trebles thee o'er makes you three times greater
Hereditary sloth natural laziness
the purpose cherish hit the nail on the head
invest clothe
Ebbing unsuccessful
setting eager expression
throes thee hurts you
weak remembrance poor memory
spirit of persuasion chatterbox
only / Professes his only job is

SEBASTIAN What? Art thou waking?
ANTONIO Do you not hear me speak?
SEBASTIAN I do, and surely
It is a sleepy language, and thou speak'st
Out of thy sleep. What is it thou didst say?
This is a strange repose, to be asleep
With eyes wide open; standing, speaking, moving,
And yet so fast asleep.
ANTONIO Noble Sebastian,
Thou let'st thy fortune sleep – die rather; wink'st
Whiles thou art waking.
SEBASTIAN Thou dost snore distinctly;
There's meaning in thy snores.
ANTONIO I am more serious than my custom. You
Must be so too, if heed me; which to do,
Trebles thee o'er.
SEBASTIAN Well: I am standing water.
ANTONIO I'll teach you how to flow.
SEBASTIAN Do so – to ebb
Hereditary sloth instructs me.
ANTONIO O!
If you but knew how you the purpose cherish
Whiles thus you mock it; how in stripping it
You more invest it. Ebbing men, indeed,
Most often do so near the bottom run
By their own fear, or sloth.
SEBASTIAN Prithee say on.
The setting of thine eye and cheek proclaim
A matter from thee; and a birth, indeed,
Which throes thee much to yield.
ANTONIO Thus, sir:
Although this lord of weak remembrance, this,
Who shall be of as little memory
When he is earthed, hath here almost persuaded –
For he's a spirit of persuasion, only
Professes to persuade – the king his son's alive,
'Tis as impossible that he's undrowned
As he that sleeps here, swims.
SEBASTIAN I have no hope
That he's undrowned.

Antonio predicts the fulfilment of Sebastian's greatest ambitions. Alonso's heir, Claribel, is so far distant that destiny itself invites Antonio and Sebastian to act. Sebastian recalls another usurpation.

---

1 Persuasion

In lines 224–8, Antonio mocked the sleeping Gonzalo, saying that persuasion is Gonzalo's only profession ('only / Professes to persuade'). But Antonio himself displays considerable powers of persuasion as he encourages Sebastian to seize the throne of Naples by murdering his brother. Antonio uses different techniques:

Certainty (lines 228–30) for all Gonzalo's cheering words, Ferdinand is dead, as sure as the sleeping Gonzalo is not swimming.

Appeal to ambition (lines 231–5) Ferdinand's death opens up the opportunity for Sebastian's highest hopes to be fulfilled.

Hyperbole (lines 238–42) with extravagant exaggeration, Antonio claims that Claribel has no hope of succeeding to Alonso's throne. She lives too far away ('beyond man's life'); only a messenger moving as fast as the sun could reach her ('unless the sun were post'); the journey would take as long as the time from a baby boy being born until he is ready to shave. Notice that, in lines 247–50, Sebastian summarises everything Antonio has said, but stripped of hyperbole.

Theatrical imagery (lines 243–6) 'cast', 'perform', 'act', 'prologue', 'discharge'; the prologue is now history, it is up to us to decide how to perform the plot.

As he senses Sebastian beginning to respond, Antonio makes his meaning plainer in lines 250–61. Write notes for the actor, suggesting how the lines could be spoken most persuasively.

---

pierce a wink...there imagine anything greater
Ten leagues thirty miles
note message
post messenger
discharge performance
cubit arm's length
There be that can rule Naples You can be king
prate chatter
amply lengthily
chough jackdaw (talking bird)
Tender like
supplant usurp, overthrow

ANTONIO O, out of that 'no hope'
What great hope have you! No hope that way is
Another way so high a hope that even
Ambition cannot pierce a wink beyond,
But doubt discovery there. Will you grant with me
That Ferdinand is drowned?
SEBASTIAN He's gone.
ANTONIO Then tell me,
Who's the next heir of Naples?
SEBASTIAN Claribel.
ANTONIO She that is Queen of Tunis; she that dwells
Ten leagues beyond man's life; she that from Naples
Can have no note, unless the sun were post –
The man i'th'moon's too slow – till new-born chins
Be rough and razorable; she that from whom
We all were sea-swallowed, though some cast again –
And by that destiny, to perform an act
Whereof what's past is prologue; what to come
In yours and my discharge.
SEBASTIAN What stuff is this? How say you?
'Tis true my brother's daughter's Queen of Tunis,
So is she heir of Naples, 'twixt which regions
There is some space.
ANTONIO A space, whose ev'ry cubit
Seems to cry out, 'How shall that Claribel
Measure us back to Naples? Keep in Tunis,
And let Sebastian wake.' Say this were death
That now hath seized them, why, they were no worse
Than now they are. There be that can rule Naples
As well as he that sleeps; lords that can prate
As amply and unnecessarily
As this Gonzalo; I myself could make
A chough of as deep chat. O, that you bore
The mind that I do! What a sleep were this
For your advancement! Do you understand me?
SEBASTIAN Methinks I do.
ANTONIO And how does your content
Tender your own good fortune?
SEBASTIAN I remember
You did supplant your brother Prospero.

Antonio points out his gains from overthrowing Prospero. He says that he has no conscience, and proposes a murderous plot. Sebastian agrees, but asks to talk further. Ariel wakens the sleepers.

---

1 Antonio – a man without a conscience

Antonio reveals that he has no conscience, and feels no sense of guilt for illegally seizing Prospero's crown. He makes his evil plan crystal clear: he will kill Alonso so that Sebastian can become king. Sebastian must kill Gonzalo to silence any criticism.

Antonio shows great contempt for the courtiers. He describes Gonzalo as 'This ancient morsel, this Sir Prudence', and dismisses the others as people who will follow any instruction, as eagerly as a cat drinks milk. They will do whatever they are ordered ('tell the clock…hour').

Antonio's language is rich in metaphor – almost every line contains a striking image. For example, 'if my conscience were like a chilblain on the heel, I'd have to wear a slipper' (lines 269–70). Work through lines 269–83, identifying the metaphors. Use the information below and at the foot of the page to help you.

image	*metaphor*
'kybe' (sore)	conscience
'deity in my bosom'	God in my heart (conscience)
'candied'	let conscience freeze
'melt…molest'	unfreeze before they hurt
'obedient steel'	dagger
'lay to bed forever'	kill
'perpetual wink for aye'	death

---

feater more elegantly
upbraid criticise
tell the clock agree
case example (usurping Prospero)
got'st gained, seized
tribute protection money
project plan, purpose

ANTONIO True;
And look how well my garments sit upon me,
Much feater than before. My brother's servants
Were then my fellows, now they are my men.
SEBASTIAN But for your conscience?
ANTONIO Ay, sir: where lies that? If 'twere a kybe
'Twould put me to my slipper; but I feel not
This deity in my bosom. Twenty consciences
That stand 'twixt me and Milan, candied be they,
And melt ere they molest. Here lies your brother,
No better than the earth he lies upon,
If he were that which now he's like – that's dead;
Whom I with this obedient steel, three inches of it,
Can lay to bed for ever: whiles you doing thus,
To the perpetual wink for aye might put
This ancient morsel, this Sir Prudence, who
Should not upbraid our course. For all the rest,
They'll take suggestion as a cat laps milk;
They'll tell the clock to any business that
We say befits the hour.
SEBASTIAN Thy case, dear friend,
Shall be my precedent. As thou got'st Milan,
I'll come by Naples. Draw thy sword; one stroke
Shall free thee from the tribute which thou payest,
And I the king shall love thee.
ANTONIO Draw together:
And when I rear my hand, do you the like
To fall it on Gonzalo.
SEBASTIAN O, but one word. [*They talk apart*]

Enter ARIEL [*invisible*] *with music*

ARIEL My master through his art foresees the danger
That you, his friend, are in, and sends me forth –
For else his project dies – to keep them living.
(*Sings in Gonzalo's ear*)
While you here do snoring lie,
Open-eyed conspiracy
His time doth take.
If of life you keep a care,
Shake off slumber and beware.
Awake, awake.

Sebastian and Antonio explain that their swords are drawn to protect the king from lions. Gonzalo tells that he was woken by a humming noise. The courtiers leave, urged by Alonso to search for Ferdinand.

Choose a suitable quotation from the scene as a caption to this picture.

1 Convincing explanations (in groups of four)

Antonio and Sebastian are caught with swords in their hands. They have to provide a plausible explanation. But do they sound convincing? Explore ways of speaking lines 301–9 to show the two conspirators struggling to sound sincere. In some productions, Sebastian makes the audience laugh at line 305 when he changes his story from 'bulls' to 'lions'.

sudden quick, violent
drawn sword in hand
securing your repose guarding your sleep
verily true

ANTONIO Then let us both be sudden.

[*Antonio and Sebastian draw their swords*]

GONZALO [*Waking*] Now, good angels preserve the king.

[*He shakes Alonso*]

ALONSO Why, how now? ho! Awake? Why are you drawn?
Wherefore this ghastly looking?

GONZALO What's the matter?

SEBASTIAN Whiles we stood here securing your repose,
Even now, we heard a hollow burst of bellowing,
Like bulls, or rather lions; did't not wake you?
It struck mine ear most terribly.

ALONSO I heard nothing.

ANTONIO O, 'twas a din to fright a monster's ear,
To make an earthquake. Sure it was the roar
Of a whole herd of lions.

ALONSO Heard you this, Gonzalo?

GONZALO Upon mine honour, sir, I heard a humming,
And that a strange one too, which did awake me.
I shaked you, sir, and cried. As mine eyes opened,
I saw their weapons drawn. There was a noise,
That's verily. 'Tis best we stand upon our guard,
Or that we quit this place. Let's draw our weapons.

ALONSO Lead off this ground, and let's make further search
For my poor son.

GONZALO Heavens keep him from these beasts:
For he is sure i'th'island.

ALONSO Lead away.

ARIEL Prospero my lord shall know what I have done.
So, king, go safely on to seek thy son.

Exeunt

Caliban curses Prospero, saying that Prospero's creatures control and torment him for the slightest offence. Fearing that Trinculo is one of Prospero's spirits, Caliban hides himself with his cloak.

---

1 Read the scene (in groups of three)

Scene 2 can be wonderfully funny in the theatre and in a reading. To gain a first impression, take parts as Caliban, Trinculo and Stephano, and read straight through. Don't pause to work out words you don't understand, but just enjoy the humour. There are serious questions to ask about the scene, but they can wait until after the first reading!

2 Scene change?

In modern theatre productions, scenes flow quickly, one after the other, without pause. If you were directing the play, would you want to give the audience some sense that the scene location has moved (for example, by a change of design or lighting)? Or would you simply show Caliban entering as soon as Alonso and the others have left the stage? Give reasons for your choice.

3 Tormenting Caliban (in groups of six to ten)

Caliban first curses Prospero, then describes the ways in which Prospero torments him for every minor offence ('every trifle'). One person takes the role of a narrator, and the others play Caliban and the spirits. The narrator slowly reads lines 1–14, pausing after each torment. In the pause, the others act out what happens to Caliban as Prospero's spirits torment him. There are at least seven torments.

Afterwards, talk together about whether or not you think that Caliban deserves to be treated harshly for such actions as 'bringing wood in slowly'.

---

flats swamps
inch-meal inch by inch
urchin-shows hedgehogs like demons
firebrand will o'the wisp
every trifle each small offence
mow make faces
wound twined about
Perchance perhaps
mind notice

Act 2 Scene 2
Near Caliban's cave

Enter CALIBAN, with a burden of wood. A noise of thunder heard

CALIBAN All the infections that the sun sucks up
From bogs, fens, flats, on Prosper fall, and make him
By inch-meal a disease. His spirits hear me,
And yet I needs must curse. But they'll nor pinch,
Fright me with urchin-shows, pitch me i'th'mire,
Nor lead me like a firebrand in the dark
Out of my way, unless he bid 'em; but
For every trifle are they set upon me,
Sometime like apes, that mow and chatter at me
And after bite me; then like hedgehogs, which
Lie tumbling in my barefoot way and mount
Their pricks at my footfall; sometime am I
All wound with adders, who with cloven tongues
Do hiss me into madness.

Enter TRINCULO

Lo, now lo!
Here comes a spirit of his, and to torment me
For bringing wood in slowly. I'll fall flat,
Perchance he will not mind me.
[*He lies down, and covers himself with a cloak*]

Trinculo, fearful of the weather, discovers Caliban, and thinks of using him to make his fortune in England. Hearing thunder, Trinculo creeps under Caliban's cloak. Stephano enters, drunk and singing.

1 Trinculo and Stephano (in pairs)

The mood of the play changes as two new characters appear, having somehow escaped from the shipwreck. Trinculo is Alonso's court jester, and Stephano is Alonso's butler (wine steward), much the worse for drink!

Experiment with ways of speaking Trinculo's lines 18–38 to make them as funny as possible. One actor who played Trinculo said: 'There are two things to remember about him. He's afraid of everything – and he pauses a lot as he works out what he's going to say or do next!'.

Stephano's bawdy song is quite unlike Ariel's music. Work out an appropriate style in which Stephano could sing.

2 'And had but this fish painted'

The Elizabethan and Jacobean exploration of the Americas is strongly echoed in *The Tempest* (see pages 154–7). Explorers sometimes brought inhabitants of the newly-discovered countries back to England. These 'Indians' were often cruelly displayed for profit in fairgrounds and other public places. A painted board would entice every 'holiday fool' to gawp at the so-called 'savages', many of whom died as a result of England's unfamiliar food and cold climate. The exhibitors made large profits from this inhuman practice ('there would this monster make a man' means make a large fortune).

3 'Strange bedfellows'?

Trinculo's 'Misery acquaints a man with strange bedfellows' has become a popular saying. Have you ever experienced a situation in which trouble has landed you in unusual company?

---

bear off protect from
bombard large leather bottle
poor-John salted fish (hake)
painted advertised (painted on a board)
doit small coin
o'my troth! by my faith
gaberdine cloak
bedfellows friends
shroud stay covered
dregs last drop
swabber deck-cleaner
tang sharp edge, serpent's tongue

TRINCULO Here's neither bush nor shrub to bear off any weather at all, and another storm brewing – I hear it sing i'th'wind. Yond same black cloud, yond huge one, looks like a foul bombard that would shed his liquor. If it should thunder as it did before, I know not where to hide my head. Yond same cloud cannot choose but fall by pailfuls. [*Sees Caliban*] What have we here – a man, or a fish? Dead or alive? A fish, he smells like a fish; a very ancient and fishlike smell; a kind of, not-of-the-newest poor-John. A strange fish. Were I in England now – as once I was – and had but this fish painted, not a holiday-fool there but would give a piece of silver. There would this monster make a man; any strange beast there makes a man. When they will not give a doit to relieve a lame beggar, they will lay out ten to see a dead Indian. Legged like a man – and his fins like arms. Warm, o'my troth! I do now let loose my opinion, hold it no longer: this is no fish, but an islander, that hath lately suffered by a thunderbolt. [*Thunder*] Alas, the storm is come again. My best way is to creep under his gaberdine; there is no other shelter hereabout. Misery acquaints a man with strange bedfellows. I will here shroud till the dregs of the storm be past.

[*He hides under Caliban's cloak*]

Enter STEPHANO [*carrying a bottle and*] *singing*

STEPHANO I shall no more to sea, to sea,
Here shall I die ashore.

This is a very scurvy tune to sing at a man's funeral. Well, here's my comfort. (*Drinks*)

(*Sings*) The master, the swabber, the boatswain and I,
The gunner and his mate,
Loved Mall, Meg, and Marian, and Margery,
But none of us cared for Kate.
For she had a tongue with a tang,
Would cry to a sailor, 'Go hang!'
She loved not the savour of tar nor of pitch,
Yet a tailor might scratch her where'er she did itch.
Then to sea, boys, and let her go hang!

This is a scurvy tune too; but here's my comfort. (*Drinks*)

CALIBAN Do not torment me! O!

Claiming to be brave, Stephano thinks of making a profit out of the four-legged 'monster'. Caliban cries out in fear. Stephano forces Caliban to drink, but is frightened by the sound of Trinculo's voice.

'Here is that which will give language to you, cat' (liquor can make a cat speak). In line 89, Stephano uses another proverb current in Shakespeare's time, 'I have no long spoon' (he who eats with the devil needs a long spoon).

1 Making a profit

Stephano, like Trinculo only moments before, thinks about how he can make a profit out of Caliban. Although Shakespeare puts these thoughts into the minds of two comic characters, he may be criticising what actually took place when the English colonised America, often treating the native inhabitants with brutal indifference (see pages 154–7).

Ind India
give ground retreat
ague fever
recover revive
neat's leather cow-hide (shoes)
anon soon
trembling (thought to be a sign of being possessed by devils)
chops jaws
detract criticise

STEPHANO What's the matter? Have we devils here? Do you put tricks upon's with savages and men of Ind? Ha? I have not 'scaped drowning to be afeared now of your four legs. For it hath been said, 'As proper a man as ever went on four legs, cannot make him give ground'; and it shall be said so again, while Stephano breathes at' nostrils.

CALIBAN The spirit torments me! O!

STEPHANO This is some monster of the isle, with four legs, who hath got, as I take it, an ague. Where the devil should he learn our language? I will give him some relief if it be but for that. If I can recover him, and keep him tame, and get to Naples with him, he's a present for any emperor that ever trod on neat's leather.

CALIBAN Do not torment me, prithee! I'll bring my wood home faster.

STEPHANO He's in his fit now, and does not talk after the wisest. He shall taste of my bottle. If he have never drunk wine afore, it will go near to remove his fit. If I can recover him, and keep him tame, I will not take too much for him; he shall pay for him that hath him, and that soundly.

CALIBAN Thou dost me yet but little hurt; thou wilt anon, I know it by thy trembling. Now Prosper works upon thee.

STEPHANO Come on your ways. Open your mouth; here is that which will give language to you, cat. Open your mouth; this will shake your shaking, I can tell you, and that soundly.

[*Caliban drinks and spits it out*]

You cannot tell who's your friend: open your chops again.

[*Caliban drinks again*]

TRINCULO I should know that voice. It should be – but he is drowned, and these are devils. O defend me!

STEPHANO Four legs and two voices; a most delicate monster! His forward voice now is to speak well of his friend; his backward voice is to utter foul speeches, and to detract. If all the wine in my bottle will recover him, I will help his ague. Come.

[*Caliban drinks*]

Amen. I will pour some in thy other mouth.

TRINCULO Stephano.

STEPHANO Doth thy other mouth call me? Mercy, mercy! This is a devil, and no monster. I will leave him; I have no long spoon.

Stephano pulls Trinculo out from under Caliban's cloak. Trinculo is delighted to find Stephano alive. Caliban thinks that Stephano is a god, and decides to become his servant.

---

1 Echoes and parallels (in small groups)

Echoes of Prospero Caliban's promise to serve Stephano loyally (lines 112–13) seems to echo what happened to Caliban when Prospero first came to the island. Then, too, Caliban was a willing servant and showed Prospero the fertile places of the island.

Echoes of history Stephano's story (lines 108–9) contains an echo of what happened during a real shipwreck, which may have inspired Shakespeare to write *The Tempest* (see pages 152–3). In that shipwreck, too, the sailors heaved the barrels overboard.

Echoes of religion Stephano's instruction to Trinculo and Caliban to 'kiss the book' (lines 117 and 128), echoes the custom of kissing the Bible when promising to tell the truth, or vowing allegiance to a lord.

Echoes of legend 'I was the man i'th'moon when time was'. Once upon a time, I was the man in the moon, says Stephano (lines 124–5). The legend was that an old man was banished to the moon for gathering wood on a Sunday. On the moon he had only his dog and a thorn bush for company. Stephano's words also echo what happened as the Americas were colonised. Some settlers pretended that they came from the moon, in an attempt to impress the native people.

These echoes may mean little to a modern audience. Consider each one in turn, and talk together about whether you think that knowing the references deepens your enjoyment of the play, or whether it's just the kind of thing you have to know for examinations!

---

siege excrement
moon-calf monster
vent excrete, throw out
not constant unsettled
sprites Prospero's spirits
celestial heavenly
butt of sack barrel of wine
kiss the book swig from the bottle (a parody of swearing an oath)

TRINCULO Stephano! If thou beest Stephano, touch me, and speak to me; for I am Trinculo – be not afeared – thy good friend Trinculo.

STEPHANO If thou beest Trinculo, come forth! I'll pull thee by the lesser legs. If any be Trinculo's legs, these are they.

[*Pulls him out*]

Thou art very Trinculo indeed! How cam'st thou to be the siege of this moon-calf? Can he vent Trinculos?

TRINCULO I took him to be killed with a thunder-stroke. But art thou not drowned, Stephano? I hope now thou art not drowned. Is the storm over-blown? I hid me under the dead moon-calf's gaberdine for fear of the storm. And art thou living, Stephano? O Stephano, two Neapolitans 'scaped!

[*Embraces Stephano*]

STEPHANO Prithee do not turn me about, my stomach is not constant.

CALIBAN [*Aside*] These be fine things, and if they be not sprites. That's a brave god, and bears celestial liquor. I will kneel to him.

STEPHANO How didst thou 'scape? How cam'st thou hither? Swear by this bottle how thou cam'st hither. I escaped upon a butt of sack which the sailors heaved o'erboard, by this bottle – which I made of the bark of a tree, with mine own hands, since I was cast ashore.

CALIBAN I'll swear upon that bottle to be thy true subject, for the liquor is not earthly.

STEPHANO Here. Swear then how thou escap'dst.

TRINCULO Swum ashore, man, like a duck. I can swim like a duck, I'll be sworn.

STEPHANO [*Gives bottle to Trinculo*] Here, kiss the book. Though thou canst swim like a duck, thou art made like a goose.

TRINCULO O Stephano, hast any more of this?

STEPHANO The whole butt, man. My cellar is in a rock by the sea-side, where my wine is hid. [*To Caliban*] How now, moon-calf, how does thine ague?

Caliban is totally in awe of Stephano, and swears obedience to him. He promises to serve Stephano by showing him the island's resources. Trinculo mocks Caliban's desire to worship a drunkard.

1 Conducted tour (in small groups)

Caliban's promises to Stephano are expressed in vivid verse. Create a presentation based on lines 146–58, in which Caliban and the others act out, as if in a dream, the exploration of the island. Caliban shows 'the best springs', plucks berries, catches fish, and so on.

2 Trinculo's mockery

Trinculo seems contemptuous of Caliban. He mocks Caliban's promise to serve the drunkard Stephano. Work out how Trinculo should speak each of his criticisms (which begin at lines 130, 136, 140, 144, 151 and 164). For example, are they asides to the audience, or does Stephano overhear some, but choose to ignore them?

In Act 3, you will find that Trinculo's clear-sighted mockery gets him into trouble.

3 'Monster' (in small groups)

Stephano and Trinculo do not see Caliban as a human being like themselves. Make a list of all the names they call Caliban in Scene 2. Add to your list as you read through the play. Count the number of times they call him 'monster'.

In one production, Caliban appeared in later scenes with a placard around his neck on which 'Monster' was written. Talk together about your thoughts on this piece of stage business.

---

when time was once upon a time
furnish it anon fill it soon
credulous gullible, foolish
drawn swallowed
sooth faith
perfidious treacherous
puppy-headed dog-brained, stupid

CALIBAN Hast thou not dropped from heaven?

STEPHANO Out o'th'moon I do assure thee. I was the man i'th'moon, when time was.

CALIBAN I have seen thee in her; and I do adore thee. My mistress showed me thee, and thy dog, and thy bush.

STEPHANO Come, swear to that! [*Giving him the bottle*] Kiss the book – I will furnish it anon with new contents. Swear.

[*Caliban drinks*]

TRINCULO [*Aside*] By this good light, this is a very shallow monster. I afeared of him? A very weak monster. The man i'th'moon? A most poor, credulous monster. Well drawn, monster, in good sooth.

CALIBAN I'll show thee every fertile inch o'th'island. And I will kiss thy foot – I prithee be my god.

TRINCULO [*Aside*] By this light, a most perfidious and drunken monster – when's god's asleep he'll rob his bottle.

CALIBAN I'll kiss thy foot; I'll swear myself thy subject.

STEPHANO Come on then: down and swear.

TRINCULO [*Aside*] I shall laugh myself to death at this puppy-headed monster. A most scurvy monster. I could find in my heart to beat him –

STEPHANO [*To Caliban*] Come, kiss.

TRINCULO – but that the poor monster's in drink. An abominable monster.

CALIBAN I'll show thee the best springs; I'll pluck thee berries;
I'll fish for thee, and get thee wood enough.
A plague upon the tyrant that I serve!
I'll bear him no more sticks, but follow thee,
Thou wondrous man.

TRINCULO [*Aside*] A most ridiculous monster, to make a wonder of a poor drunkard.

Caliban continues with his promise to serve Stephano and to share with him the secret resources of the island. Stephano decides to become king of the island. Caliban sings about his freedom from Prospero.

---

1 From servant to servant (in groups of three)

Many productions use Caliban's song as an opportunity for a joyous exit from the stage. Very often, Stephano and Trinculo join in the singing. But Caliban's shout of 'freedom' is ironic, since he has simply exchanged one master for another. Stage the final moments of the scene to show as clearly as possible that Caliban has not found freedom, but has just become the slave of a different master.

2 Three drunkards

By the end of this scene, all three characters are likely to be very drunk. Stephano, the 'drunken butler', had a head start with the wine he salvaged from the shipwreck. Trinculo's name is very much like *trincone*, the Italian for a drunkard. Caliban has had his first taste of alcohol, and it has probably had a devastating effect.

It is very difficult for an actor to play the part of a drunkard convincingly. Below are some actors' tips for imitating a drunk. Use the advice to try out different ways of performing the scene. Think about whether you want to make the audience laugh at Caliban, or to feel sorry for him, as he becomes the worse for drink.

> Imagine your left foot is nailed to the floor. Try to walk in all directions with the other. Remember that drunks have terrible difficulty in focusing and in hearing. Struggle with your words, but remember that you have to make them perfectly clear to the audience, even if you slur them. So, take your time, and make it seem as if you are searching slowly for each word in your mind, and having difficulty finding them!

---

crabs crab apples
pig-nuts ground nuts
marmoset small monkey
clust' ring filberts bunches of nuts
scamels (sea birds?) no one really knows what Shakespeare meant, so make your own guess
firing firewood
scrape trenchering scrub wooden plates
high-day liberty, holiday

CALIBAN I prithee let me bring thee where crabs grow;
And I with my long nails will dig thee pig-nuts,
Show thee a jay's nest, and instruct thee how
To snare the nimble marmoset. I'll bring thee
To clust'ring filberts, and sometimes I'll get thee
Young scamels from the rock. Wilt thou go with me?

STEPHANO I prithee, now lead the way without any more talking. Trinculo, the king and all our company else being drowned, we will inherit here. [*To Caliban*] Here; bear my bottle. Fellow Trinculo, we'll fill him by and by again.

CALIBAN (*Sings drunkenly*) Farewell, master; farewell, farewell.

TRINCULO A howling monster; a drunken monster.

CALIBAN [*Singing*] No more dams I'll make for fish,
Nor fetch in firing
At requiring,
Nor scrape trenchering, nor wash dish,
Ban, ban, Ca-caliban
Has a new master – get a new man.

Freedom, high-day, high-day freedom, freedom high-day, freedom.

STEPHANO O brave monster, lead the way!

Exeunt

Looking back at Act 2

Activities for groups or individuals

1 Where the place?

The location of Prospero's island is never given in the play, although clues are scattered throughout Acts 1 and 2. Milan, Naples, Tunis, Carthage, the Mediterranean and Algiers are all mentioned, as are 'the still-vexed (always stormy) Bermudas'. There seems little point in trying to locate the island, because it exists in the imagination. But what kind of place is it?

Design a simple set to suggest the various locations where the action takes place, so that scene changes can be made quickly.

2 The ship's passengers – and crew

By the end of Act 2, three groups of the shipwrecked court party have been clearly established:

Alonso and the courtiers (who are wandering on the island)
Stephano and Trinculo (who have met up with Caliban)
Ferdinand (who has fallen in love with Miranda).

Make a map of the shipwreck, showing how Ferdinand and the others reached the shore, and what has happened to them so far. Don't forget to include the crew and the ship. Add appropriate quotations to your map.

3 Dramatic irony? (in small groups)

Scene 1 reveals the murderous intentions of the 'civilised' Antonio and Sebastian. Scene 2, which shows Caliban's encounter with Stephano and Trinculo, reflects what happened when Europeans colonised the Americas. The Europeans assumed that they were superior to the native people, tried to make money out of them, drugged them with alcohol, and made them their servants.

Talk together about whether or not you think Shakespeare is using Act 2 to make ironic and critical comments on colonisation and 'civilisation' (use pages 154–7 to help you).

4 Where is Prospero?

Prospero does not appear in Act 2. Imagine that he makes a brief appearance in Scenes 1 and 2 to comment on the action. Write six to eight lines for him for each scene.

The Tempest in modern dress. The play has been set in many periods. In this production, Alonso and Gonzalo are talking together on the left. Contrast the presentation of the two mocking and evil-intentioned aristocrats on the right with the photograph on page 46, which shows a production in more traditional costumes.

Ferdinand reflects that his hard labour is pleasurable, because thoughts of Miranda make the work enjoyable. Miranda pleads with him to rest. She says that the logs will weep for Ferdinand as they burn.

'Work not so hard.' Prospero forces Ferdinand to do exactly the same wood-carrying task as Caliban. But Ferdinand claims that he enjoys his hard labour, because he thinks about Miranda while he works.

1 Contrasts

Lines 1–9 contain at least eight contrasts. Read the lines aloud, using your hands as a pair of scales to 'weigh out' the contrasts and comparisons (for example, 'sport' versus 'painful', 'labour' versus 'delight', and so on).

sets off cancels
baseness hard labour
odious hateful
quickens brings to life
crabbed harsh and irritable
sore injunction strict command
such baseness…like executor such low-grade work never had so noble a workman
Most busy…do it Miranda fills my mind as I work
enjoined ordered, forced

ACT 3 SCENE 1
Near Prospero's cave

Enter FERDINAND, bearing a log

FERDINAND [*Sets down the log*] There be some sports are painful, and their labour
Delight in them sets off. Some kinds of baseness
Are nobly undergone; and most poor matters
Point to rich ends. This my mean task
Would be as heavy to me as odious, but
The mistress which I serve quickens what's dead,
And makes my labours pleasures. O, she is
Ten times more gentle than her father's crabbed –
And he's composed of harshness. I must remove
Some thousands of these logs, and pile them up,
Upon a sore injunction. My sweet mistress
Weeps when she sees me work, and says such baseness
Had never like executor. I forget. [*Picks up the log*]
But these sweet thoughts do even refresh my labours,
Most busy, least when I do it.

Enter MIRANDA, *and* PROSPERO [*following at a distance*]

MIRANDA Alas, now pray you
Work not so hard. I would the lightning had
Burnt up those logs that you are enjoined to pile.
Pray set it down, and rest you. When this burns
'Twill weep for having wearied you. My father
Is hard at study; pray now, rest yourself –
He's safe for these three hours.

Miranda wants to carry the logs, but Ferdinand prevents her. Prospero observes that Miranda is in love. Ferdinand declares his love for her. He says that, of all the women he has known, Miranda is without equal.

---

1 Catching the plague of love

Prospero's lines 31–2 compare falling in love with catching a disease ('visitation' means visit of the plague). A modern equivalent is 'you've got it bad'. But why does Prospero call his daughter 'Poor worm'? Think of one or two possible reasons.

2 'Admired Miranda'

Miranda disobeys her father's order and tells Ferdinand her name. In Latin, Miranda means 'to be wondered at'. Ferdinand plays with this meaning in 'admired' and 'admiration' (lines 38–9). If you turn back to the young lovers' first meeting, you will find that Ferdinand calls her 'O you wonder' (Act 1 Scene 2, line 425). Think about what Miranda's name suggests to you about her appearance and her character.

3 Absolute sincerity (in pairs)

This is what one actor who played Ferdinand said about lines 38–49:

> Ferdinand has been captivated by many women, but found some fault in every one. Only Miranda is perfect. You have to play these lines absolutely sincerely, full of wonder. Although it's not the kind of language you hear nowadays, you can make it ring true. Your job is to convince the audience you are really in love for the first time. You simply mustn't be embarrassed. The same applies to Miranda's lines too!

Take the actor's advice as your cue to practise speaking as Ferdinand and Miranda.

---

crack strain
become me suit
infected in love ('you've caught it')
visitation visit (like a disease)
hest command
into bondage…ear captured me (made me fall in love)
too diligent over-attentive
foil contrast
peerless without equal

FERDINAND O most dear mistress,
The sun will set before I shall discharge
What I must strive to do.
MIRANDA If you'll sit down
I'll bear your logs the while. Pray give me that;
I'll carry it to the pile.
FERDINAND No, precious creature,
I'd rather crack my sinews, break my back,
Than you should such dishonour undergo,
While I sit lazy by.
MIRANDA It would become me
As well as it does you; and I should do it
With much more ease, for my good will is to it,
And yours it is against.
PROSPERO [*Aside*] Poor worm, thou art infected;
This visitation shows it.
MIRANDA You look wearily.
FERDINAND No, noble mistress, 'tis fresh morning with me
When you are by at night. I do beseech you
Chiefly, that I might set it in my prayers,
What is your name?
MIRANDA Miranda. – O my father,
I have broke your hest to say so.
FERDINAND Admired Miranda,
Indeed the top of admiration, worth
What's dearest to the world. Full many a lady
I have eyed with best regard, and many a time
Th'harmony of their tongues hath into bondage
Brought my too diligent ear. For several virtues
Have I liked several women, never any
With so full soul but some defect in her
Did quarrel with the noblest grace she owed,
And put it to the foil. But you, O you,
So perfect and so peerless, are created
Of every creature's best.

Miranda declares her love for Ferdinand, and he describes how he fell in love with her at first sight. He professes his overwhelming love for her. Miranda weeps, and Prospero blesses their love.

---

1 How many children had Lady Macbeth?

The Shakespeare critic, L.C. Knights, wrote a famous essay entitled 'How many children had Lady Macbeth?' In it, he mocked the way in which some people approach a study of Shakespeare's plays by asking literal questions. He wanted the plays to be treated as dramatic poems, which can be enjoyed for the beauty of their verse and for their imaginative power.

This imaginative approach to Shakespeare can help you with some of the puzzles which appear in *The Tempest*. For example, in line 50, Miranda says that she cannot remember any women's faces, even though in Act 1 Scene 2, line 47, she remembered several women. Similarly, she says she has seen only two men (lines 51–3), even though in Act 1 Scene 2, line 444, she spoke of three men.

Imagine that you are teaching the play, and one of your students asks you if Shakespeare had made mistakes here (and at page 36, activity 1), or forgotten what he had written earlier. What will you reply?

2 Images

Which of the following images do you find easy to visualise? Put them in order, ranging from the easiest to the most difficult.

'The jewel in my dower' (line 55)
'This wooden slavery' (line 64)
'The flesh-fly blow my mouth' (line 65)
'My heart fly to your service' (line 67)
'patient log-man' (line 69)
'Heavens rain grace / On that which breeds between 'em' (lines 77–8)

---

glass mirror
How features are abroad what men look like elsewhere
skilless ignorant
The jewel in my dower my most precious possession
precepts orders
wooden slavery log-carrying
blow foul
kind event happy outcome
if hollowly, invert...mischief if I lie, change my good fortune to bad

MIRANDA I do not know
One of my sex; no woman's face remember,
Save from my glass, mine own. Nor have I seen
More that I may call men than you, good friend,
And my dear father. How features are abroad
I am skilless of; but by my modesty,
The jewel in my dower, I would not wish
Any companion in the world but you;
Nor can imagination form a shape
Besides yourself, to like of. But I prattle
Something too wildly, and my father's precepts
I therein do forget.
FERDINAND I am in my condition
A prince, Miranda; I do think a king –
I would not so – and would no more endure
This wooden slavery than to suffer
The flesh-fly blow my mouth. Hear my soul speak.
The very instant that I saw you, did
My heart fly to your service, there resides
To make me slave to it, and for your sake
Am I this patient log-man.
MIRANDA Do you love me?
FERDINAND O heaven, O earth, bear witness to this sound,
And crown what I profess with kind event
If I speak true; if hollowly, invert
What best is boded me to mischief. I,
Beyond all limit of what else i'th'world,
Do love, prize, honour you.
MIRANDA I am a fool
To weep at what I'm glad of.
PROSPERO [*Aside*] Fair encounter
Of two most rare affections. Heavens rain grace
On that which breeds between 'em.
FERDINAND Wherefore weep you?

Miranda indirectly explains her tears, then openly says she wants to marry Ferdinand. He willingly agrees. Prospero expresses pleasure. In Scene 2, Trinculo comments sceptically on his and his companions' intelligence.

---

1 An image of fertility

In lines 79–83, Miranda explains in an enigmatic way why she is weeping. She then decides to speak directly ('this is trifling', 'Hence, bashful cunning') and offers herself as wife to Ferdinand.

Some critics have noted that Miranda uses an image of pregnancy to describe her way of speaking initially in riddles: 'the more it seeks to hide itself / The bigger bulk it shows'. Although this may seem an unlikely image for the innocent Miranda to use, it looks forward to the masque in Act 4, with its images of fertility and harvest. Keep the image in mind as you read on.

2 'A thousand thousand'

Advise the actor playing Ferdinand what action he could use at line 93 to emphasise his words.

3 Staging Scene 2 (in groups of three)

Take parts and read through Scene 2. All three men have been drinking heavily, and can probably barely stand. Work out how you would stage the scene, identifying the lines where you would attempt to get the loudest laughs from the audience. For example, Trinculo's sceptical statement, 'if th'other two be brained like us, the state totters', usually gains a great response.

---

want lack
trifling playing with words
maid servant
fellow companion
As bondage…freedom as ever a prisoner greeted freedom
appertaining relating to this
butt is out barrel is empty
bear up, and board 'em drink up (sailors' toast, like 'cheers')
brained like as intelligent as

MIRANDA At mine unworthiness, that dare not offer
What I desire to give, and much less take
What I shall die to want. But this is trifling,
And all the more it seeks to hide itself
The bigger bulk it shows. Hence, bashful cunning,
And prompt me, plain and holy innocence.
I am your wife, if you will marry me;
If not, I'll die your maid. To be your fellow
You may deny me, but I'll be your servant
Whether you will or no.
FERDINAND [*Kneeling*] My mistress, dearest,
And I thus humble ever.
MIRANDA My husband then?
FERDINAND Aye, with a heart as willing
As bondage e'er of freedom. Here's my hand.
MIRANDA And mine, with my heart in't; and now farewell
Till half an hour hence.
FERDINAND A thousand thousand.
Exeunt Ferdinand and Miranda [*separately*]
PROSPERO So glad of this as they I cannot be,
Who are surprised with all; but my rejoicing
At nothing can be more. I'll to my book,
For yet ere supper-time must I perform
Much business appertaining. *Exit*

Act 3 Scene 2
Near Caliban's cave

Enter CALIBAN, STEPHANO and TRINCULO

STEPHANO Tell not me. When the butt is out we will drink water, not a drop before; therefore bear up, and board 'em. Servant monster, drink to me.

TRINCULO [*Aside*] Servant monster? The folly of this island! They say there's but five upon this isle; we are three of them – if th'other two be brained like us, the state totters.

Stephano promises to make Caliban his deputy. Caliban accuses Trinculo of cowardice, and is mocked in return. Stephano threatens to hang Trinculo for mutiny. Ariel begins to create trouble for Trinculo.

Stephano, Trinculo and Caliban. Choose a line from Scene 2 to make a suitable caption for this moment.

1 Trinculo the critic

Although Trinculo is also drunk, he seems to have a clear-sighted view of his companions. Each time he speaks in lines 4–30, he ridicules the others, often by using puns. Work out a piece of stage business for Trinculo for each of his speeches, so that his actions help the audience's understanding.

set fixed, staring
five and thirty leagues over a hundred miles
standard standard-bearer (or able to stand)
list please (or keel over like a sinking ship)
in case ready (brave enough)
deboshed drunken, lecherous
quoth he he says
natural idiot
subject servant
suit proposition, request
Marry by Saint Mary

STEPHANO Drink, servant monster, when I bid thee; thy eyes are almost set in thy head.

TRINCULO Where should they be set else? He were a brave monster indeed if they were set in his tail.

STEPHANO My man-monster hath drowned his tongue in sack. For my part, the sea cannot drown me – I swam, ere I could recover the shore, five and thirty leagues off and on. By this light, thou shalt be my lieutenant, monster, or my standard.

TRINCULO Your lieutenant if you list; he's no standard.

STEPHANO We'll not run, monsieur monster.

TRINCULO Nor go neither; but you'll lie like dogs, and yet say nothing neither.

STEPHANO Moon-calf, speak once in thy life, if thou beest a good moon-calf.

CALIBAN How does thy honour? Let me lick thy shoe. I'll not serve him, he is not valiant.

TRINCULO Thou liest, most ignorant monster; I am in case to jostle a constable. Why, thou deboshed fish thou, was there ever man a coward that hath drunk so much sack as I today? Wilt thou tell a monstrous lie, being but half a fish, and half a monster?

CALIBAN Lo, how he mocks me. Wilt thou let him, my lord?

TRINCULO 'Lord', quoth he? That a monster should be such a natural!

CALIBAN Lo, lo again! Bite him to death, I prithee.

STEPHANO Trinculo, keep a good tongue in your head. If you prove a mutineer, the next tree. The poor monster's my subject, and he shall not suffer indignity.

CALIBAN I thank my noble lord. Wilt thou be pleased to hearken once again to the suit I made to thee?

STEPHANO Marry will I. Kneel, and repeat it. I will stand, and so shall Trinculo.

Enter ARIEL *invisible*

CALIBAN As I told thee before, I am subject to a tyrant, a sorcerer, that by his cunning hath cheated me of the island.

ARIEL Thou liest.

CALIBAN [*To Trinculo*] Thou liest, thou jesting monkey thou. I would my valiant master would destroy thee. I do not lie.

Stephano threatens Trinculo. Caliban begs Stephano to kill Prospero. Ariel gets Trinculo into further trouble by again imitating his voice. Stephano beats Trinculo.

1 Comic echoes

The three drunken characters provide a comic parody of one of the main themes of the play: usurpation (the overthrow of a rightful ruler). Stephano tries to behave like a king, and demands that his subjects obey him. He even threatens to hang Trinculo if he mutinies ('the next tree'). Caliban's plot to overthrow Prospero is a comic reflection of the way in which Antonio seized the throne of Milan from Prospero, and of the conspiracy to kill Alonso. Even Stephano's threat to Trinculo, 'I will supplant some of your teeth' (line 45), echoes the theme of usurpation ('supplant' means uproot).

Already imagining that he is king of the island, Stephano strikes Trinculo at line 70. But poor Trinculo gets his beating for something he hasn't done! Stephano thinks Trinculo is mocking him, but Ariel is really to blame.

a Invent a gesture for Stephano as he says 'the next tree' (line 33).

b Trinculo blames his beating on drink ('this can sack and drinking do' means 'this is what wine makes you do'). In some productions, Trinculo speaks lines 72–4 angrily, in others sulkily, in others fearfully, afraid of another beating. How would you advise the actor playing Trinculo to deliver the lines?

2 'Thou liest'

Ariel gets Trinculo into trouble by imitating his voice at lines 41, 58 and 69. Work out how Ariel moves, how close he stands to Trinculo, and how he behaves after he has spoken. Your aim is to increase the comic effect of the scene. For example, in one production, Ariel leapt on to Trinculo's back and stayed there until line 70.

Mum then hush!
compassed brought about
pied ninny many-coloured fool
patch jester's costume
brine salt water
quick freshes fresh water springs
stockfish dried cod (softened by beating)
pox curse
murrain plague

STEPHANO Trinculo, if you trouble him any more in's tale, by this hand, I will supplant some of your teeth.

TRINCULO Why, I said nothing.

STEPHANO Mum then, and no more. [*To Caliban*] Proceed.

CALIBAN I say by sorcery he got this isle;
From me he got it. If thy greatness will
Revenge it on him – for I know thou dar'st,
But this thing dare not –

STEPHANO That's most certain.

CALIBAN Thou shalt be lord of it, and I'll serve thee.

STEPHANO How now shall this be compassed? Canst thou bring me to the party?

CALIBAN Yea, yea, my lord, I'll yield him thee asleep,
Where thou mayst knock a nail into his head.

ARIEL Thou liest, thou canst not.

CALIBAN What a pied ninny's this? [*To Trinculo*] Thou scurvy patch!
[*To Stephano*] I do beseech thy greatness give him blows,
And take his bottle from him. When that's gone,
He shall drink nought but brine, for I'll not show him
Where the quick freshes are.

STEPHANO Trinculo, run into no further danger. Interrupt the monster one word further, and by this hand, I'll turn my mercy out o'doors, and make a stockfish of thee.

TRINCULO Why, what did I? I did nothing. I'll go farther off.

STEPHANO Didst thou not say he lied?

ARIEL Thou liest.

STEPHANO Do I so?

[*Strikes Trinculo*]

Take thou that! As you like this, give me the lie another time.

TRINCULO I did not give the lie. Out o'your wits, and hearing too? A pox o'your bottle! This can sack and drinking do. A murrain on your monster, and the devil take your fingers!

CALIBAN Ha, ha, ha!

STEPHANO Now forward with your tale. [*To Trinculo*] Prithee stand further off.

CALIBAN Beat him enough; after a little time
I'll beat him too.

Caliban proposes a plan to kill Prospero. Stephano agrees to do the deed, and says that he will take Miranda as his queen, and make Trinculo and Caliban his deputies.

---

1 Another plot! (in pairs)

Caliban's plot has clear parallels with both the conspiracy of Antonio and Alonso against Prospero, and Antonio and Sebastian's plot against Alonso. Notice how Caliban urges Stephano to burn the books which give Prospero his magical powers. The same books probably led to Prospero's overthrow as Duke of Milan, because he was so busy studying them that he neglected state affairs.

Experiment with different ways of speaking lines 81–97 to give them as much dramatic impact as possible.

2 Truth telling

'They all do hate him / As rootedly as I', says Caliban, claiming that Prospero's spirits loathe their master. Do you think Caliban is telling the truth?

3 Advise the actor

Advise the actor playing Trinculo how to speak his one word 'Excellent' (line 104), in reply to Stephano's question as to whether he likes the plot. In the 1993 Royal Shakespeare Company production, Trinculo stretched it out very slowly and sarcastically 'Ex–cell–ent'. Do you think that Trinculo's reply is sarcastic, or spoken in some other way?

4 Dramatic contrast

Lines 99–102 make a stark contrast with the tender love scene between Ferdinand and Miranda. Suggest the effect you would try to create with these lines if you were directing the play.

---

paunch him stab him in the stomach
wezand windpipe, throat
sot drunkard, fool
brave utensils household goods
deck decorate
nonpareil without equal in beauty
dam mother
brave brood many children
viceroys deputies to the king
jocund happy
troll the catch sing the song loudly
but whilere just now

STEPHANO Stand farther. [*To Caliban*] Come, proceed.
CALIBAN Why, as I told thee, 'tis a custom with him
I'th'afternoon to sleep. There thou mayst brain him,
Having first seized his books; or with a log
Batter his skull, or paunch him with a stake,
Or cut his wezand with thy knife. Remember
First to possess his books; for without them
He's but a sot, as I am, nor hath not
One spirit to command – they all do hate him
As rootedly as I. Burn but his books;
He has brave utensils – for so he calls them –
Which when he has a house, he'll deck withal.
And that most deeply to consider, is
The beauty of his daughter. He himself
Calls her a nonpareil. I never saw a woman
But only Sycorax my dam, and she;
But she as far surpasseth Sycorax
As great'st does least.
STEPHANO Is it so brave a lass?
CALIBAN Ay, lord, she will become thy bed, I warrant,
And bring thee forth brave brood.
STEPHANO Monster, I will kill this man. His daughter and I will be king and queen – save our graces! – and Trinculo and thyself shall be viceroys. Dost thou like the plot, Trinculo?
TRINCULO Excellent.
STEPHANO Give me thy hand. I am sorry I beat thee. But while thou liv'st, keep a good tongue in thy head.
CALIBAN Within this half hour will he be asleep,
Wilt thou destroy him then?
STEPHANO Ay, on mine honour.
ARIEL This will I tell my master.
CALIBAN Thou mak'st me merry. I am full of pleasure,
Let us be jocund. Will you troll the catch
You taught me but whilere?

The three drunkards sing raucously, but Ariel's music strikes fear into Stephano and Trinculo. Caliban urges them not to be afraid, and describes delightful sounds and wonderful dreams. They follow Ariel's music.

---

1 Raucous singing (in groups of three)

The three characters 'troll the catch' (roar out the song). A 'catch' is a round, in which each person starts singing at a different point. Work out your own version of the song, and try singing it.

2 Caliban's dream (in small groups)

Stephano and Trinculo appear terror-stricken by Ariel's music. But Caliban tells them about the delightful noises of the island and his wonderful dreams. Choose one or more of the following activities on Caliban's lines 130–8:

a Choral speaking
Devise a way of speaking the lines so that everyone in the group shares them. Use echoes and repetitions.

b Sound effects
Experiment with ways of accompanying Caliban's words with sound effects. For example, Caliban could pause frequently to listen. Fill the pauses with what he hears.

c Different emotional tones
Explore ways of speaking the lines in different tones of voice. For example, try speaking full of wonder and awe, sadly, and so on.

d Conversation or soliloquy?
Caliban's words are spoken to Stephano, but could they be just as effective as a soliloquy? Speak the lines as if they were part of a conversation, then as a soliloquy which Caliban either addresses to the audience or speaks to himself.

---

reason performance
Flout 'em, and scout 'em mock them and jeer at them
tabor drum
Nobody the invisible man
thou beest you are
list wish, please
airs tunes
lays it on plays the drum splendidly

STEPHANO At thy request, monster, I will do reason, any reason. Come on, Trinculo, let us sing.

They sing Flout 'em, and scout 'em
And scout 'em, and flout 'em.
Thought is free.

CALIBAN That's not the tune.

Ariel plays the tune on a tabor and pipe

STEPHANO What is this same?

TRINCULO This is the tune of our catch, played by the picture of Nobody.

STEPHANO If thou beest a man, show thyself in thy likeness: if thou beest a devil, take't as thou list.

TRINCULO O forgive me my sins!

STEPHANO He that dies pays all debts! I defy thee! Mercy upon us!

CALIBAN Art thou afeared?

STEPHANO No, monster, not I.

CALIBAN Be not afeared, the isle is full of noises,
Sounds, and sweet airs, that give delight and hurt not.
Sometimes a thousand twangling instruments
Will hum about mine ears; and sometime voices,
That if I then had waked after long sleep,
Will make me sleep again; and then in dreaming,
The clouds methought would open, and show riches
Ready to drop upon me, that when I waked
I cried to dream again.

STEPHANO This will prove a brave kingdom to me, where I shall have my music for nothing.

CALIBAN When Prospero is destroyed.

STEPHANO That shall be by an by: I remember the story.

[*Exit Ariel, playing music*]

TRINCULO The sound is going away; let's follow it, and after do our work.

STEPHANO Lead, monster, we'll follow. I would I could see this taborer, he lays it on.

TRINCULO [*To Caliban*] Wilt come? I'll follow Stephano.

Exeunt

Gonzalo and Alonso are wearied by their wanderings. Alonso gives up hope of finding Ferdinand alive. Sebastian and Antonio again plot to murder Alonso. A banquet magically appears.

1 A moral maze?

Some critics argue that lines 2–3 symbolise the spiritual journey of King Alonso. He is wandering in a labyrinth ('maze'), unable to find his way out. As you read on, keep in mind the idea of Alonso travelling on a symbolic journey, on which he learns, through suffering, to repent his wrong-doings.

However, Antonio and Sebastian remain unchanged. Once again, they plan to murder Alonso. Think about how lines 11–17 could be played to emphasise the contrast between the villainy of Antonio and Sebastian, and the vulnerability of Alonso and Gonzalo.

2 Stage directions (in small groups)

Every production of the play tries to present the stage directions following lines 17 and 19 as dramatically as possible. Select a place in your school or college, and work out how you could stage your own presentation there. Consider each of the following stage directions in turn:

'*Solemn and strange music*' compose your own music
'PROSPERO *on the top*' how could this be shown?
'*invisible*' how would you suggest Prospero's invisibility?
'*Enter several strange shapes*' costumes? appearance? (see also page 103)
'*bringing in a banquet*' design the banquet (it is on a table, see the stage directions at lines 52 and 82)
'*dance about it*' invent the dance around the banquet
'*with gentle actions of salutations*' how do they salute the king?
'*inviting the King, etc. to eat*' what are the gestures and movements?
'*they depart*' devise a dramatic departure.

By'r lakin by our Lady (the Virgin Mary)
forth-rights and meanders straight and winding paths
attached seized
frustrate vain, useless
for one repulse because of our first failure
the purpose the murder
advantage opportunity
throughly thoroughly
travail travel-weariness

Act 3 Scene 3
A remote part of the island

Enter ALONSO, SEBASTIAN, ANTONIO, GONZALO, ADRIAN, FRANCISCO and others

GONZALO By'r lakin, I can go no further, sir,
My old bones aches. Here's a maze trod indeed
Through forth-rights and meanders. By your patience,
I needs must rest me.
ALONSO Old lord, I cannot blame thee,
Who am myself attached with weariness
To th'dulling of my spirits. Sit down, and rest.
Even here I will put off my hope, and keep it
No longer for my flatterer. He is drowned
Whom thus we stray to find, and the sea mocks
Our frustrate search on land. Well, let him go.
ANTONIO [*Drawing Sebastian aside*] I am right glad that he's so out of hope.
Do not for one repulse forgo the purpose
That you resolved t'effect.
SEBASTIAN [*To Antonio*] The next advantage
Will we take throughly.
ANTONIO Let it be tonight;
For now they are oppressed with travail, they
Will not, nor cannot use such vigilance
As when they're fresh.
SEBASTIAN I say tonight: no more.

Solemn and strange music, and [*enter*] PROSPERO *on the top, invisible*

ALONSO What harmony is this? my good friends, hark!
GONZALO Marvellous sweet music.

Enter several strange shapes, bringing in a banquet, and dance about it with gentle actions of salutations, and inviting the King, etc. to eat, they depart

The courtiers wonder at what they have seen, saying it resembled something from mythology or travellers' tales. Prospero comments on the evil of Alonso, Sebastian and Antonio, and hints at further marvels.

---

1 Travellers' tales

Lines 20–49 are rich in echoes of the fantasies of fable and mythology, and the travellers' tales which the early explorers brought home. The following will help your understanding:

'unicorn' (line 22) A mythical horse with a long, spiked horn.

'phoenix' (lines 22–4) A fabulous bird. Only one lived at any time. It burned itself upon a funeral pyre ('throne'), and arose, new-born, from the ashes.

'Travellers ne'er did lie' (lines 26–7) Explorers brought back seemingly incredible stories of what they had seen in distant lands. Their fantastic stories were often ridiculed.

'Dewlapped like bulls' (lines 44–6) People living in mountain regions often developed goitres (large swellings beneath the chin).

'such men' (lines 46–7) Travellers reported that they had seen men whose heads were in their chests ('the anthropophagi' of *Othello*, Act 1 Scene 3, lines 143–4).

'Each putter-out of five for one' (line 48) In Shakespeare's time, explorers could finance their expeditions by betting on the likelihood of their success. They deposited a sum of money before they left. If they returned safely, they could claim five times their deposit.

Almost every line opposite (except Prospero's) contains an expression of wonder or disbelief. Pick out a word or phrase in each line which each actor could emphasise to express a sense of wonder.

---

kind keepers guardian angels
drollery puppet show
want credit lack credibility
certes certainly
muse marvel at
Praise in departing there's more to come! (don't praise until you've seen it all)
viands food
Good warrant of true stories

ALONSO Give us kind keepers, heavens! What were these?
SEBASTIAN A living drollery! Now I will believe
That there are unicorns; that in Arabia
There is one tree, the phoenix' throne, one phoenix
At this hour reigning there.
ANTONIO I'll believe both;
And what does else want credit, come to me
And I'll be sworn 'tis true. Travellers ne'er did lie,
Though fools at home condemn 'em.
GONZALO If in Naples
I should report this now, would they believe me?
If I should say I saw such islanders –
For certes, these are people of the island –
Who though they are of monstrous shape, yet note
Their manners are more gentle, kind, than of
Our human generation you shall find
Many, nay almost any.
PROSPERO [*Aside*] Honest lord,
Thou hast said well – for some of you there present
Are worse then devils.
ALONSO I cannot too much muse,
Such shapes, such gesture, and such sound, expressing –
Although they want the use of tongue – a kind
Of excellent dumb discourse.
PROSPERO [*Aside*] Praise in departing.
FRANCISCO They vanished strangely.
SEBASTIAN No matter, since they
Have left their viands behind; for we have stomachs.
Wilt please you taste of what is here?
ALONSO Not I.
GONZALO Faith, sir, you need not fear. When we were boys,
Who would believe that there were mountaineers,
Dewlapped like bulls, whose throats had hanging at 'em
Wallets of flesh? Or that there were such men
Whose heads stood in their breasts? Which now we find
Each putter-out of five for one will bring us
Good warrant of.

Alonso, Sebastian and Antonio prepare to eat, but the banquet vanishes. Disguised as a harpy, Ariel accuses the three men of overthrowing Prospero, and calls on them to repent. Ariel then vanishes.

'*Enter* ARIEL, like a harpy.' A harpy was a fabulous monster in Greek mythology. It had the head and torso of a woman, and the tail, wings and talons of a bird. Design your own version of Ariel's appearance as a harpy.

1 Ariel's accusation

After accusing the men of sin, Ariel declares them unfit to live. He reminds them of their powerlessness, of their overthrow of Prospero, and of the ruin they now face as a result. Ariel tells them that only sorrowful repentance and virtuous living can save them now ('heart's sorrow, / And a clear life ensuing').

Practise ways of speaking Ariel's lines to greatest dramatic effect.

to instrument control over
lower world earth
never-surfeited ever hungry
suchlike valour foolish bravery
tempered made hard
dowl tiny feather
plume plumage
fellow ministers spirits
massy heavy
requit avenged
powers divine rulers
Ling'ring perdition slow ruin

ALONSO I will stand to, and feed, although my last;
No matter, since I feel the best is past.
Brother, my lord the duke, stand to and do as we.

Thunder and lightning. Enter ARIEL, *like a harpy, claps his wings upon the table, and with a quaint device the banquet vanishes*

ARIEL You are three men of sin, whom Destiny –
That hath to instrument this lower world,
And what is in't – the never-surfeited sea
Hath caused to belch up you. And on this island,
Where man doth not inhabit – you 'mongst men
Being most unfit to live – I have made you mad;
And even with suchlike valour men hang and drown
Their proper selves.
[*Alonso, Sebastian, etc. draw their swords*]
You fools! I and my fellows
Are ministers of Fate. The elements
Of whom your swords are tempered may as well
Wound the loud winds, or with bemocked-at stabs
Kill the still-closing waters, as diminish
One dowl that's in my plume. My fellow ministers
Are like invulnerable. If you could hurt,
Your swords are now too massy for your strengths,
And will not be uplifted. But remember –
For that's my business to you – that you three
From Milan did supplant good Prospero;
Exposed unto the sea – which hath requit it –
Him, and his innocent child; for which foul deed,
The powers, delaying, not forgetting, have
Incensed the seas and shores, yea, all the creatures
Against your peace. Thee of thy son, Alonso,
They have bereft; and do pronounce by me
Ling'ring perdition – worse than any death
Can be at once – shall step by step attend
You, and your ways; whose wraths to guard you from –
Which here, in this most desolate isle, else falls
Upon your heads – is nothing but heart's sorrow,
And a clear life ensuing.

Prospero congratulates Ariel. Alonso, remorseful, decides to drown himself. Sebastian and Antonio leave to fight the spirits. Gonzalo says all three feel guilty and sends the younger courtiers after them.

1 What a performance!

Ariel has performed excellently ('bravely'), and Prospero's other spirit servants ('meaner ministers') have also put on a splendid spectacle ('with good life / And observation strange' means vividly and imaginatively). But just what did the 'shapes' (spirits) do in support of Ariel?

Write notes for the actors playing Prospero's spirit servants, advising them on costume, movements, and on what they should do in their presentation to Alonso, Sebastian and Antonio. It seems that each spirit does something different, using its particular talents ('several kinds').

2 Feelings of guilt (in small groups)

Prospero's plan is working. Alonso feels that he stands accused by all of Nature: 'billows' (waves), 'winds' and 'thunder'. He now feels a great sense of guilt for wronging Prospero, and thinks his punishment is that his own son, Ferdinand, has drowned. Alonso decides that death by drowning must also be his destiny. But Sebastian and Antonio determine to resist. They have no words expressing guilt, only a desire to fight.

Talk together about whether you think Sebastian and Antonio should show any acknowledgement of guilt (for example, in a long pause before speaking line 102). Give reasons for your decision.

mocks and mows insulting gestures and faces
figure part
devouring completely
bated omitted
bass my trespass loudly sing my wrong-doing
i'th'ooze is bedded lies in the mud of the sea-bed
plummet sounded plumb-line measured
of suppler joints younger
ecstasy madness

Ariel vanishes in thunder; then, to soft music, enter the shapes again, and dance, with mocks and mows, and [then depart] carrying out the table

PROSPERO Bravely the figure of this harpy hast thou
Performed, my Ariel; a grace it had devouring.
Of my instruction hast thou nothing bated
In what thou hadst to say. So, with good life
And observation strange, my meaner ministers
Their several kinds have done. My high charms work,
And these, mine enemies, are all knit up
In their distractions. They now are in my power;
And in these fits I leave them, while I visit
Young Ferdinand, whom they suppose is drowned,
And his and mine loved darling.

GONZALO I'th'name of something holy, sir, why stand you
In this strange stare?

ALONSO O, it is monstrous: monstrous!
Methought the billows spoke and told me of it,
The winds did sing it to me, and the thunder,
That deep and dreadful organ-pipe, pronounced
The name of Prosper. It did bass my trespass;
Therefore my son i'th'ooze is bedded; and
I'll seek him deeper than e'er plummet sounded,
And with him there lie mudded. *Exit*

SEBASTIAN But one fiend at a time,
I'll fight their legions o'er.

ANTONIO I'll be thy second.
Exeunt Sebastian and Antonio

GONZALO All three of them are desperate. Their great guilt,
Like poison given to work a great time after,
Now 'gins to bite the spirits. I do beseech you,
That are of suppler joints, follow them swiftly,
And hinder them from what this ecstasy
May now provoke them to.

ADRIAN Follow, I pray you.
Exeunt

Looking back at Act 3

Activities for groups or individuals

1 Conscience-stricken (in small groups)

Alonso's conscience is aroused as he listens to Ariel reminding him of his part in Prospero's overthrow. But neither Antonio nor Sebastian seem to feel regret or remorse. Talk together about whether you feel there are some people who do not feel repentant for their crimes, however strongly they are reminded of them.

2 Different views of the island

Write a sentence which begins 'I see this island as…' for each of the following at this point in the play:

Prospero, Miranda, Caliban, Ariel, Alonso, Antonio, Ferdinand, Stephano, Trinculo, Gonzalo.

3 Stage directions

Remind yourself of all the stage directions in Scene 3. Use them as the basis for designing a cover for an edition of the play.

4 Poetry and prose

As a general rule in Shakespeare, high status characters speak in verse, and comic or low status characters speak in prose. But, in Scene 2 lines 130–8, the low-status Caliban speaks some of Shakespeare's greatest poetry.

Check quickly through the play, identifying who speaks prose, and on which occasions. Suggest why they do so.

5 Three scenes, three minutes

Devise a mini-version of Act 3, expressing the essence of each scene in one minute. By way of preparation, you may find it helpful to read through the synopsis of the action at the top of each left-hand page.

Remember that, in Act 3, the characters are in a state of altered consciousness. Ferdinand and Miranda are in love; Stephano, Trinculo and Caliban have been drinking heavily; and the courtiers witness a fantastic spectacle, and say that they are willing to believe anything.

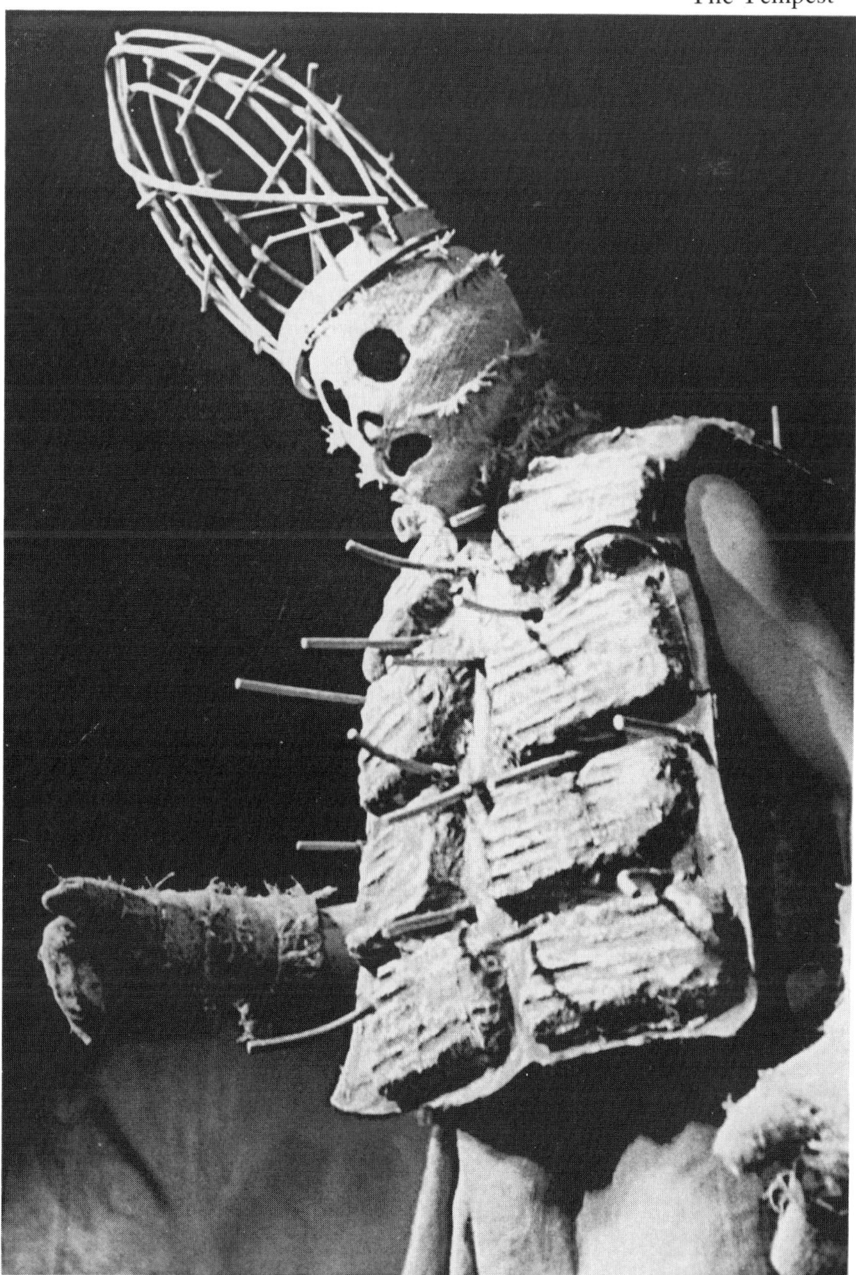

Ariel's fellow spirits appear as '*strange shapes*' in Scene 3. They dance, 'make gentle actions of salutations', pull faces ('mocks and mows'), and bring on the banquet. This photograph shows how the shapes were presented by the Royal Shakespeare Company, 1963. Design your own costumes for the 'strange shapes'.

Prospero tells Ferdinand that he has successfully endured the testing of his love, and can therefore marry Miranda. But Prospero warns against sex before marriage: it will bring misery.

---

1 'A third of mine own life' (in pairs)

Once again Shakespeare provides a challenge to the imagination. If Miranda is, for Prospero, 'a third of mine own life', what could form the other two-thirds? No one knows for sure, and various suggestions have been made, such as Milan and his books, or his marriage, or thirty years of his life (Miranda is fifteen).

What do you think are the other 'thirds' which Prospero has in mind? Make your own suggestions.

2 Convincing a modern audience

In lines 14–22, Prospero warns Ferdinand not to have sexual intercourse with Miranda before they marry. If he does so, discord and hatred will follow. You will find that Prospero repeats the warning later on in the scene.

Many people think that Prospero's words show that *The Tempest* was specially performed at the wedding celebrations of Princess Elizabeth, daughter of King James I, in 1612–13. In those days, the belief that premarital sex is undesirable was much stronger than it is today.

Imagine that you are directing the play. The actor playing Prospero writes you a private note: 'I have problems with this speech, because today many people find it unbelievable. I don't want to make the audience laugh, but I just don't believe what I'm saying here. Can you write me a paragraph or two to help me, please?' Write your reply.

---

austerely severely
tender to thy hand give you
trials tests
strangely wonderfully
ratify confirm
halt lag, limp
against an oracle even if a prophet denied it
virgin-knot virginity, chastity
sanctimonious sacred
aspersion blessing (like rain on crops)
Hymen Greek god of marriage (who carried a lamp)

ACT 4 SCENE 1
Near Prospero's cave

Enter PROSPERO, FERDINAND and MIRANDA

PROSPERO [*To Ferdinand*] If I have too austerely punished you
Your compensation makes amends, for I
Have given you here a third of mine own life,
Or that for which I live; who once again
I tender to thy hand. All thy vexations
Were but my trials of thy love, and thou
Hast strangely stood the test. Here, afore heaven,
I ratify this my rich gift. O Ferdinand,
Do not smile at me, that I boast her of,
For thou shalt find she will outstrip all praise
And make it halt behind her.

FERDINAND I do believe it against an oracle.

PROSPERO Then, as my gift, and thine own acquisition
Worthily purchased, take my daughter. But
If thou dost break her virgin-knot before
All sanctimonious ceremonies may
With full and holy rite be ministered,
No sweet aspersion shall the heavens let fall
To make this contract grow; but barren hate,
Sour-eyed disdain and discord shall bestrew
The union of your bed with weeds so loathly
That you shall hate it both. Therefore take heed,
As Hymen's lamps shall light you.

Ferdinand says that he will never do anything to dishonour his marriage with Miranda. Prospero sends Ariel to arrange another dramatic spectacle, then again warns Ferdinand against passion.

1 **A second warning** (in small groups)

Ferdinand promises to keep his passions under control. Nothing must spoil his wedding day, which will seem slow-moving ('Phoebus' steeds are foundered' means 'the sun-god's horses have stopped'), making night itself seem 'chained' (unable to arrive). But, only thirty lines later, Prospero again tells Ferdinand to keep his sexual desires in check ('Do not give dalliance / Too much the rein').

Why does Prospero deliver this second warning? It might be because of something Ferdinand and Miranda are doing. Or, it might be that Prospero is behaving as an over-protective father, who is suspicious of even the most innocent behaviour.

Talk together about whether you think something in Prospero's character provokes this second warning, or whether Ferdinand and Miranda are giving 'dalliance the rein': perhaps locked in passionate embrace. In your view, which seems the more likely?

2 **'Do you love me master? No?'** (in pairs)

The relationship between Prospero and Ariel is one of the many intriguing puzzles in *The Tempest*. They are master and servant, but how do they feel towards each other?

Advise the actor playing Ariel how to speak line 48, for example, sadly, fearfully, genuinely wishing to know the answer, playfully, or in some other manner. Also decide how you think Prospero speaks line 49, 'Dearly, my delicate Ariel'. Give reasons for your decision in each case.

fair issue beautiful children
oppòrtune appropriate (for seduction)
worser genius bad angel
edge sexual pleasure
potent powerful
meaner fellows fellow spirits
the rabble fellow spirits
Some vanity of mine art a magical illusion
Presently? immediately?
mop and mow gestures and grimaces
conceive understand

FERDINAND As I hope
For quiet days, fair issue, and long life,
With such love as 'tis now, the murkiest den,
The most oppòrtune place, the strong'st suggestion
Our worser genius can, shall never melt
Mine honour into lust, to take away
The edge of that day's celebration,
When I shall think or Phoebus' steeds are foundered,
Or night kept chained below.
PROSPERO Fairly spoke.
Sit then, and talk with her, she is thine own.
What, Ariel! My industrious servant Ariel!

Enter ARIEL

ARIEL What would my potent master? Here I am.
PROSPERO Thou and thy meaner fellows your last service
Did worthily perform; and I must use you
In such another trick. Go bring the rabble –
O'er whom I give thee power – here, to this place.
Incite them to quick motion, for I must
Bestow upon the eyes of this young couple
Some vanity of mine art. It is my promise,
And they expect it from me.
ARIEL Presently?
PROSPERO Ay: with a twink.
ARIEL Before you can say 'come' and 'go',
And breathe twice, and cry 'so, so',
Each one tripping on his toe,
Will be here with mop and mow.
Do you love me master? No?
PROSPERO Dearly, my delicate Ariel. Do not approach
Till thou dost hear me call.
ARIEL Well; I conceive. *Exit*
PROSPERO [*To Ferdinand*] Look thou be true! Do not give dalliance
Too much the rein. The strongest oaths are straw
To th'fire i'th'blood. Be more abstemious,
Or else good night your vow.

Ferdinand promises that his love will overcome his lust. The masque begins. Iris describes Ceres' fertility, and commands her to join Juno in celebration. Ceres asks why she must obey.

1 The masque

Masques were spectacular court entertainments, rich in elaborate scenery and gorgeous costumes. They were very expensive affairs. King James I spent £20,000 on one masque (over £1 million today). Filled with music, poetry and dance, masques revelled in visual effects. Complex stage machinery and lighting created striking illusions. The masque which Prospero has arranged for Ferdinand and Miranda symbolises two major themes of *The Tempest*:

Harmony after the storm The appearance of Iris, goddess of the rainbow, expresses the peace which follows a tempest. Just as a rainbow appears after a storm, so Iris herself is an emblem of Prospero's plan: the wedding of Ferdinand and Miranda which will harmoniously unite Milan and Naples after many years of trouble.

Notice the way in which Iris is likened to the rainbow: 'watery arch', 'many-coloured', 'blue bow', 'Rich scarf'.

Bounty and fertility Ceres, goddess of harvest, symbolises the riches that will result from the wedding of Ferdinand and Miranda. In lines 60–9, Iris describes the fertile natural world over which Ceres reigns.

Read through Iris' description, a section at a time (there are six sections, each beginning with the word 'Thy'). After reading each section, close your eyes and try to conjure up a picture of what Iris describes: crops ('vetches' means beans); mountains and sheep-filled meadows ('leas', 'meads'); flowery river banks ('pionèd and twillèd'); shady woods; pruned ('pole-clipped') vineyards; the seashore ('sea-marge').

liver sexual desire
a corollary too many
want lack
stover hay
hest command
broom-groves gorse thickets, woods
dismissèd bachelor jilted lover
lass-lorn without a lover
dost air relax
amain speedily
saffron yellow
bosky acres woods

FERDINAND I warrant you, sir,
The white cold virgin snow upon my heart
Abates the ardour of my liver.

PROSPERO Well.
Now come, my Ariel – bring a corollary,
Rather than want a spirit; appear, and pertly.

Soft music

No tongue! All eyes! Be silent!

THE MASQUE

Enter IRIS

IRIS Ceres, most bounteous lady, thy rich leas
Of wheat, rye, barley, vetches, oats and peas;
Thy turfy mountains, where live nibbling sheep,
And flat meads thatched with stover, them to keep;
Thy banks with pionèd and twillèd brims,
Which spongy April at thy hest betrims
To make cold nymphs chaste crowns; and thy broom-groves,
Whose shadow the dismissèd bachelor loves,
Being lass-lorn; thy pole-clipped vineyard,
And thy sea-marge, sterile and rocky-hard,
Where thou thyself dost air: the queen o'th'sky,
Whose watery arch and messenger am I,
Bids thee leave these, and with her sovereign grace,
Here on this grass-plot, in this very place
To come and sport. Her peacocks fly amain.
Approach, rich Ceres, her to entertain.

Enter CERES

CERES Hail, many-coloured messenger, that ne'er
Dost disobey the wife of Jupiter;
Who, with thy saffron wings, upon my flowers
Diffusest honey drops, refreshing showers,
And with each end of thy blue bow dost crown
My bosky acres, and my unshrubbed down,
Rich scarf to my proud earth. Why hath thy queen
Summoned me hither, to this short-grazed green?

Iris tells Ceres that they are meeting to celebrate a wedding. She assures Ceres that Venus and Cupid will not be present, and that they have failed to bewitch Ferdinand and Miranda. Juno and Ceres sing a blessing.

---

1 Classical mythology

Like most Jacobean masques, Prospero's masque draws heavily upon classical mythology. Imagine that you have been asked to write some notes for a theatre programme to help a modern audience. Use the information given on pages 108 and 112, and an encyclopedia or book on classical mythology. Write brief notes on each of the following: Iris, Ceres, Juno, Venus, Cupid, Hymen and Proserpine (Persephone). Suggest how each has a special symbolic significance in *The Tempest*.

2 What happens in the masque?

The following will help you understand the sequence of the masque:

lines 60–9 Iris praises Ceres' bountifulness
lines 70–4 Iris summons Ceres to join Juno to 'sport'
lines 76–83 Ceres praises Iris and asks why Juno has summoned her
lines 84–6 Iris says that the celebration is for Ferdinand and Miranda's forthcoming wedding
lines 86–91 Ceres fears that Venus may join the celebrations
lines 91–101 Iris assures Ceres that Venus and Cupid will not be present, and that they have been unsuccessful in their plot to make Ferdinand and Miranda misbehave sexually
lines 101–9 Juno arrives and sings her blessing on the marriage
lines 110–17 Ceres blesses Ferdinand and Miranda, promising them rich harvest
lines 128–38 Iris calls the nymphs and harvesters to dance.

---

estate bestow
Venus goddess of love
dusky Dis Pluto, god of the Underworld
scandalled improper
her deity Venus
Paphos town in Cyprus, centre of Venus-worship
wanton charm wicked spell
bed-right sexual intercourse
hot minion lustful favourite
gait walk
issue children
foison abundance
garners grain stores

IRIS A contract of true love to celebrate,
And some donation freely to estate
On the blest lovers.
CERES Tell me, heavenly bow,
If Venus or her son, as thou dost know,
Do now attend the queen? Since they did plot
The means that dusky Dis my daughter got,
Her and her blind boy's scandalled company
I have forsworn.
IRIS Of her society
Be not afraid. I met her deity
Cutting the clouds towards Paphos, and her son
Dove-drawn with her. Here thought they to have done
Some wanton charm upon this man and maid,
Whose vows are, that no bed-right shall be paid
Till Hymen's torch be lighted – but in vain.
Mars's hot minion is returned again;
Her waspish-headed son has broke his arrows,
Swears he will shoot no more, but play with sparrows,
And be a boy right out.

[JUNO *descends*]

Highest queen of state,
Great Juno comes, I know her by her gait.
JUNO How does my bounteous sister? Go with me
To bless this twain, that they may prosperous be,
And honoured in their issue.
[*Singing*] Honour, riches, marriage-blessing,
Long continuance, and increasing,
Hourly joys be still upon you,
Juno sings her blessings on you.
[CERES] [*Singing*] Earth's increase, and foison plenty,
Barns and garners never empty,
Vines, with clust'ring bunches growing,
Plants, with goodly burden bowing;
Spring come to you at the farthest,
In the very end of harvest.
Scarcity and want shall shun you,
Ceres' blessing so is on you.

Prospero says that the spirits are enacting his fantasies. Ferdinand is full of happy wonder. Harvesters and nymphs dance at Iris' command, but are ordered off by Prospero when he remembers Caliban's plot.

The masque, Royal Shakespeare Company, 1993. Iris (messenger of the gods, the rainbow, signifying that the tempest is over and peace reigns), Juno (a moon goddess and protector of women) and Ceres (goddess of fertility, signifying rich harvests and healthy children).

1 An interrupted dance

The dance of the harvesters ('sicklemen') and nymphs ('naiads' means 'water spirits') also symbolises the theme of fertility and fruitfulness which runs throughout the masque. But in the 1993 Royal Shakespeare Company production, the dance was given an ominous twist. The three straw-hatted sicklemen danced, hiding their faces from the audience. Suddenly they looked up and revealed themselves as Caliban, Stephano and Trinculo! Talk together about what you think of this effect.

confines prisons
marred spoiled
windring brooks winding streams
sedged crowns crowns made of reeds
crisp rippling
temperate chaste, cold
furrow harvest field
footing dancing
properly habited appropriately dressed
Avoid! leave instantly!
heavily sorrowfully

FERDINAND This is a most majestic vision, and
Harmonious charmingly. May I be bold
To think these spirits?
PROSPERO Spirits, which by mine art
I have from their confines called to enact
My present fancies.
FERDINAND Let me live here ever;
So rare a wondered father, and a wife,
Makes this place paradise.

Juno and Ceres whisper, and send Iris on employment

PROSPERO Sweet now, silence.
Juno and Ceres whisper seriously,
There's something else to do. Hush, and be mute,
Or else our spell is marred.
IRIS You nymphs called naiads of the windring brooks,
With your sedged crowns, and ever-harmless looks,
Leave your crisp channels, and on this green land
Answer your summons, Juno does command.
Come, temperate nymphs, and help to celebrate
A contract of true love. Be not too late.

Enter certain nymphs

You sun-burned sicklemen of August weary,
Come hither from the furrow, and be merry,
Make holiday; your rye-straw hats put on,
And these fresh nymphs encounter every one
In country footing.

Enter certain reapers, properly habited. They join with the nymphs, in a graceful dance, towards the end whereof Prospero starts suddenly and speaks

PROSPERO [*Aside*] I had forgot that foul conspiracy
Of the beast Caliban and his confederates
Against my life. The minute of their plot
Is almost come. [*To the spirits*] Well done! Avoid! No more.

To a strange, hollow and confused noise [*the spirits*] *heavily vanish*

The lovers comment on Prospero's anger. Prospero tells Ferdinand not to be troubled, because everything in the masque is ephemeral, and will fade. Prospero questions Ariel about Caliban and his accomplices.

---

1 Why is Prospero angry?

Imagine that a fellow student asks you:

> Prospero is a magician, able to control the elements and command the spirit world. Yet the thought of Caliban's plot deeply troubles him. Why is he unable to control Caliban and the foolish Stephano and Trinculo?

Make your reply. (If you need help, turn to page 164.)

2 An elegy for the world? (in small groups)

Lines 148–58 ('Our revels…sleep') are full of words with strong theatrical associations: 'revels', 'actors', 'baseless fabric' (like the temporary scenery for a pageant play), 'globe', 'pageant', 'rack' (clouds painted on scenery). Just as the actors have vanished into thin air, so too will everyone and everything else.

The lines have become famous as a metaphor for the impermanence of human life. All our achievements, even the world itself, will eventually come to nothing. The mood is elegiac (an elegy is a mournful or reflective poem or song).

Talk together about why you think Prospero becomes so elegiac here. Then work out different ways in which to present the lines. One version might show how the actor could deliver Prospero's lines on stage, as part of a performance. Suggest his tone of voice, which words he should emphasise, where he could pause, and so on.

A second version could be a choral reading, in which several voices speak together. Use repetitions and echoes, together with mime and other dramatic actions, to accompany the voices.

---

distempered lacking reason
movèd sort troubled state
baseless fabric flimsy structure
all which it inherit all who live there now and later
rack tiny cloud
cleave to unite with
presented acted, introduced (see page 160)
varlets villains

FERDINAND This is strange. Your father's in some passion
That works him strongly.
MIRANDA Never till this day
Saw I him touched with anger, so distempered.
PROSPERO You do look, my son, in a movèd sort,
As if you were dismayed. Be cheerful, sir,
Our revels now are ended; these our actors,
As I foretold you, were all spirits, and
Are melted into air, into thin air;
And like the baseless fabric of this vision,
The cloud-capped towers, the gorgeous palaces,
The solemn temples, the great globe itself,
Yea, all which it inherit, shall dissolve,
And like this insubstantial pageant faded
Leave not a rack behind. We are such stuff
As dreams are made on; and our little life
Is rounded with a sleep. Sir, I am vexed.
Bear with my weakness, my old brain is troubled.
Be not disturbed with my infirmity.
If you be pleased, retire into my cell,
And there repose. A turn or two I'll walk
To still my beating mind.
FERDINAND *and* MIRANDA We wish your peace
Exeunt Ferdinand and Miranda
PROSPERO [*Summoning Ariel*] Come with a thought! – [*To Ferdinand and Miranda*] I thank thee. – Ariel, come!

Enter ARIEL

ARIEL Thy thoughts I cleave to. What's thy pleasure?
PROSPERO Spirit,
We must prepare to meet with Caliban.
ARIEL Ay, my commander. When I presented Ceres
I thought t'have told thee of it, but I feared
Lest I might anger thee.
PROSPERO Say again, where didst thou leave these varlets?

Ariel describes how he led Caliban, Stephano and Trinculo into a stinking pool. Prospero plans to punish them further, and reflects that Caliban is unteachable. Ariel hangs up gaudy clothes as a trap.

---

1 Tormenting the conspirators (in small groups)

Choose one of the following activities on Ariel's tale of how he tormented the conspirators (lines 171–84):

a One person reads Ariel's lines slowly, and the others mime each action.

b Speak aloud only two or three words from each line. Choose the words which you feel convey most powerfully what happened to the conspirators.

2 Nature versus nurture (in pairs)

Prospero's lines 188–90 echo a major theme of the play: can nurture (education, civilisation) change nature? Prospero regrets that, in spite of all his training and art, he has been unable to improve Caliban's nature ('a born devil'). He has succeeded in educating Miranda, but has failed with Caliban. So, Prospero decides that he must further punish Caliban and the others ('plague them all, / Even to roaring').

This is what one student said of lines 188–90:

> Prospero's words ('on whose nature, / Nurture can never stick') have been thought to be the key to the play. But Prospero's view of 'nurture' is a limited one. He has training as a servant in mind for Caliban, not real education. Also, you can never be sure what 'nature' is. So you can never call someone a 'born devil', because you just don't know what nature people are born with.

Talk together about how far you agree with this student's view. You will find more on the 'nature versus nurture' theme on pages 149–50.

---

valour false bravery
bending aiming
tabor drum
unbacked colts unbroken (never-ridden) horses
lowing music
filthy mantled scum covered
trumpery flashy clothes (the '*glistering apparel*' of line 193)
stale decoy, con-trick
jack knave, will-o'-the-wisp

ARIEL I told you, sir, they were red-hot with drinking,
So full of valour that they smote the air
For breathing in their faces, beat the ground
For kissing of their feet; yet always bending
Towards their project. Then I beat my tabor,
At which like unbacked colts they pricked their ears,
Advanced their eyelids, lifted up their noses
As they smelt music. So I charmed their ears
That calf-like they my lowing followed, through
Toothed briars, sharp furzes, pricking gorse, and thorns,
Which entered their frail shins. At last I left them
I'th'filthy mantled pool beyond your cell,
There dancing up to th'chins, that the foul lake
O'er-stunk their feet.

PROSPERO This was well done, my bird!
Thy shape invisible retain thou still.
The trumpery in my house, go bring it hither
For stale to catch these thieves.

ARIEL I go, I go. *Exit*

PROSPERO A devil, a born devil, on whose nature
Nurture can never stick; on whom my pains
Humanely taken, all, all lost, quite lost;
And, as with age his body uglier grows,
So his mind cankers. I will plague them all,
Even to roaring.

Enter ARIEL, *laden with glistering apparel, etc*

Come, hang them on this line.
[*Prospero and Ariel stand apart*]

Enter CALIBAN, STEPHANO *and* TRINCULO, *all wet*

CALIBAN Pray you tread softly, that the blind mole may not hear a foot fall. We now are near his cell.

STEPHANO Monster, your fairy, which you say is a harmless fairy, has done little better than played the jack with us.

TRINCULO Monster, I do smell all horse-piss, at which my nose is in great indignation.

STEPHANO So is mine. Do you hear, monster? If I should take a displeasure against you, look you –

Trinculo and Stephano complain about losing their wine, but Caliban urges them to commit the murder. The gaudy clothes attract the drunkards' interest, much to Caliban's dismay.

---

1 Playing for laughs (in groups of three)

Trinculo's repeated 'O King Stephano' (lines 220 and 224) echo a song which was popular in Shakespeare's time:

> King Stephen was a worthy peer,
> His breeches cost him but a crown,
> He held them sixpence all too dear
> Therefore he called the tailor lowne (fool).

Like Trinculo, Stephano is fascinated by the gaudy clothes, and all thoughts of murder disappear from his mind. Only Caliban recognises that the clothes are cheap junk.

The two Europeans are fooled by appearances. Their jokes about 'line' are often lost on audiences today. Perhaps lines 233–6 refer to crossing the equator, which was known as 'the Line'. Sailors sometimes shaved passengers' heads in the ceremony of 'crossing the Line'. Sometimes sailors' hair fell out as a result of a tropical disease. Alternatively, Stephano's words can be interpreted quite literally, as if he is speaking to the clothes line.

Whatever the possibilities, actors face the problem of how to make the incident with the clothes amusing for a modern audience. How would you do it? Work out how to play lines 220–52 to greatest comic effect.

2 Sympathy for Caliban?

Caliban may be unteachable, but he is quite capable of recognising a fool when he sees one in action. If you were directing the play, would you try to enlist the audience's sympathy for Caliban here?

---

hoodwink this mischance compensate for this accident
fetch off rescue
be o'er ears drown
good mischief murder
peer lord
frippery old clothes shop
dropsy disease (excess of fluids)
dote thus on be infatuated with
luggage junk
jerkin short jacket

TRINCULO Thou wert but a lost monster.

CALIBAN Good my lord, give me thy favour still.
Be patient, for the prize I'll bring thee to
Shall hoodwink this mischance. Therefore speak softly –
All's hushed as midnight yet.

TRINCULO Ay, but to lose our bottles in the pool!

STEPHANO There is not only disgrace and dishonour in that, monster, but an infinite loss.

TRINCULO That's more to me than my wetting. Yet this is your harmless fairy, monster.

STEPHANO I will fetch off my bottle, though I be o'er ears for my labour.

CALIBAN Prithee, my king, be quiet. Seest thou here,
This is the mouth o'th'cell. No noise, and enter.
Do that good mischief which may make this island
Thine own for ever, and I, thy Caliban,
For aye thy foot-licker.

STEPHANO Give me thy hand. I do begin to have bloody thoughts.

TRINCULO O King Stephano, O peer, O worthy Stephano! Look what a wardrobe here is for thee.

CALIBAN Let it alone, thou fool, it is but trash.

TRINCULO O ho, monster! We know what belongs to a frippery. [*Puts on a garment*] O King Stephano!

STEPHANO Put off that gown, Trinculo! By this hand I'll have that gown.

TRINCULO Thy grace shall have it.

CALIBAN The dropsy drown this fool! What do you mean
To dote thus on such luggage? Let't alone,
And do the murder first. If he awake,
From toe to crown he'll fill our skins with pinches,
Make us strange stuff.

STEPHANO Be you quiet, monster! Mistress line, is not this my jerkin? [*He takes the garment from the tree*] Now is the jerkin under the line. Now, jerkin, you are like to lose your hair, and prove a bald jerkin.

Despite Caliban's warning, Stephano and Trinculo are distracted by the gaudy clothes. Disguised spirits drive the conspirators away. Prospero says his enemies are in his power. He promises freedom to Ariel.

Hunting the conspirators. Every production works out its own unique way of enacting the stage direction at line 252. This German production used a crocodile rather than dogs to chase Caliban, Stephano and Trinculo.

1 Staging the pursuit

Every director has to decide how amusing to make this hunting episode. The incident recalls a terrible feature of the early colonisation of the Americas, when the Spanish settlers would sometimes hunt the natives using dogs. How would you stage the pursuit?

line and level according to rule (plumb-line and spirit-level)
pass of pate thrust of wit (wisecrack)
lime sticky substance
barnacles wild geese (in legend, geese grew from barnacles)
lay to hold out
diverse various
Mountain, Silver, Fury, Tyrant dogs' names
pard leopard

TRINCULO Do, do; we steal by line and level, and't like your grace.

STEPHANO I thank thee for that jest; here's a garment for't. Wit shall not go unrewarded while I am king of this country. 'Steal by line and level' is an excellent pass of pate: there's another garment for't.

TRINCULO Monster, come put some lime upon your fingers, and away with the rest.

CALIBAN I will have none on't. We shall lose our time,
And all be turned to barnacles, or to apes
With foreheads villainous low.

STEPHANO Monster, lay to your fingers. Help to bear this away where my hogshead of wine is, or I'll turn you out of my kingdom. [*Loading Caliban with garments*] Go to, carry this.

TRINCULO And this.

STEPHANO Ay, and this.

A noise of hunters heard. Enter diverse spirits in shape of dogs and hounds, hunting them about, Prospero and Ariel setting them on

PROSPERO Hey, Mountain, hey!

ARIEL Silver! There it goes, Silver.

PROSPERO Fury, Fury! There, Tyrant, there! Hark, hark!

[*Exeunt Caliban, Stephano and Trinculo, pursued by spirits*]

[*To Ariel*] Go, charge my goblins that they grind their joints
With dry convulsions, shorten up their sinews
With agèd cramps, and more pinch-spotted make them,
Than pard, or cat-o'-mountain.

ARIEL Hark, they roar.

PROSPERO Let them be hunted soundly. At this hour
Lies at my mercy all mine enemies.
Shortly shall all my labours end, and thou
Shalt have the air at freedom. For a little
Follow, and do me service.

Exeunt

Looking back at Act 4

Activities for groups or individuals

1 Fathers and daughters – who chooses the husband?

Prospero is the last in a long line of fathers in Shakespeare's plays who seek to control their daughters' choice of husband: Capulet in *Romeo and Juliet*, Baptista in *The Taming of the Shrew*, the Duke of Milan in *The Two Gentlemen of Verona*, Egeus in *A Midsummer Night's Dream*, Leonato in *Much Ado About Nothing*, Polonius in *Hamlet*, Lear in *King Lear*, Brabantio in *Othello* and Cymbeline in *Cymbeline.*

Shakespeare himself had two daughters, and it seems likely that he strongly disapproved of the man who married his younger daughter, Judith.

One person steps into role as William Shakespeare. The others question him about why he returns to the father–daughter theme so frequently in his plays.

2 Cheerful?

Immediately before Prospero speaks some of the best-known lines written by Shakespeare (Act 4, Scene 1, lines 148–58 'Our revels…sleep'), he says 'Be cheerful, sir' (line 147). One student wrote:

> This is very strange, because the lines are very pessimistic indeed. They say that everything will simply disappear without trace, and that our short lives don't really mean anything at all. It's like the effects of a worldwide nuclear explosion, everything will be destroyed. How can that possibly make anybody cheerful? It depresses me terribly. What's the point of anything if he means what he says?

Write a reply to this point of view.

3 Staging the masque

Talk together about how you would stage the masque. Most productions try to match the formal, ceremonial style of the language with similarly formal costumes, gestures and staging. But don't be afraid to explore.

One production chose to present the masque as a rock opera, although critics felt that such a presentation undermined the essential seriousness of this part of the play. Do you agree with the critics' view?

'O King Stephano, O peer, O worthy Stephano!' Trinculo and Stephano are fooled by the gaudy costumes. Compare this picture with the way in which Stephano and Trinculo are presented on pages 86 and 120.

Prospero foresees the success of his scheme. Ariel reports the troubled state of the king and courtiers, and expresses compassion for them. Moved by Ariel's feelings, Prospero says that he, too, will pity them.

1 Alchemy – '*magic robes*'

Lines 1–2 contain images from alchemy, an early science which attempted to change base metal into gold. An alchemist carried out a 'project' (experiment), which would 'gather to a head' (come to the boil) if it did not 'crack' (fail). The metaphor of alchemy reinforces the idea of Prospero as a magician. Turn to the picture on page 165 to see if it matches your impression of Prospero in his magic robes.

2 Prospero's project

Prospero's project seems to have a number of aims:

political (1) uniting Naples and Milan through the marriage of Ferdinand and Miranda; (2) Prospero regaining his dukedom
revenge the punishment of Alonso, Sebastian and Antonio
repentance bringing the 'three men of sin' to repent of their wrong-doings
reform overcoming, with nurture, the wicked nature of others
self-knowledge deepening Prospero's humanity by overcoming his own nature, and putting mercy before vengeance
reward releasing Ariel from his service
escape leaving the island to return to Milan
harmony achieving unity and peace in personal, social and natural life.

Present Prospero's aims as a diagram showing the relationships between them, and which aims you think are the most important. Add other aims if you wish, or invent different descriptions for each aim.

project plan
Time…carriage time moves easily, free of burdens
line-grove clump of lime trees
weather-fends protects
abide…distracted are all mad
eaves of reeds thatched roofs
kindlier more humanly, more generously

ACT 5 SCENE 1
Near Prospero's cave

Enter PROSPERO in his magic robes, and ARIEL

PROSPERO Now does my project gather to a head.
My charms crack not, my spirits obey, and Time
Goes upright with his carriage. How's the day?
ARIEL On the sixth hour; at which time, my lord,
You said our work should cease.
PROSPERO I did say so,
When first I raised the tempest. Say, my spirit,
How fares the king and's followers?
ARIEL Confined together
In the same fashion as you gave in charge,
Just as you left them; all prisoners, sir,
In the line-grove which weather-fends your cell;
They cannot budge till your release. The king,
His brother, and yours, abide all three distracted,
And the remainder mourning over them,
Brim full of sorrow and dismay; but chiefly
Him that you termed, sir, the good old lord Gonzalo.
His tears runs down his beard like winter's drops
From eaves of reeds. Your charm so strongly works 'em
That if you now beheld them, your affections
Would become tender.
PROSPERO Dost thou think so, spirit?
ARIEL Mine would, sir, were I human.
PROSPERO And mine shall.
Hast thou, which art but air, a touch, a feeling
Of their afflictions, and shall not myself,
One of their kind, that relish all as sharply
Passion as they, be kindlier moved than thou art?

Prospero decides on mercy rather than vengeance. He appeals to the spirits who have helped him to perform miracles, and declares that he will give up his magic powers.

---

1 Virtue, not vengeance (in small groups)

In *The Tempest*, the word 'virtue' has many associations: mercy, forgiveness, magnanimity, humanity, love, reason, good faith. Prospero decides that, in spite of all the injustices ('high wrongs') done to him, he will practise virtue, not vengeance. It is the nobler ('rarer') action.

Is there an inevitability about Prospero's decision? Could his nature (and the play itself) have led him to choose vengeance? Talk together about whether you think that, at the start of the play, Prospero had forgiveness or vengeance as his aim.

2 Shakespeare as Prospero?

Prospero's lines 33–57 are a kind of invocation or spell. He appeals to magical forces, and declares that he will give up his supernatural powers and become merely human again. He calls to his various spirit helpers, and names all the astonishing things they have enabled him to perform: dimming the sun, creating tempests, lightning and earthquakes, and bringing the dead back to life. He then renounces his magic powers ('this rough magic / I here abjure').

Many people believe that the lines represent Shakespeare's farewell to the theatre. For example, 'I'll drown my book' could mean 'I'll end my playwriting'. One production even presented Prospero looking just like Shakespeare!

Experiment with different ways of delivering the lines to bring out the spell-like qualities, as well as the importance of Prospero's decision to give up his magic.

---

th'quick the most tender part
sole drift single aim
ebbing Neptune retreating tide
demi-puppets tiny spirits
green sour ringlets 'fairy rings' in grass
solemn curfew bell that signals night has come
azured vault blue sky
rifted split
bolt thunderbolt
spurs roots
airy charm music

Though with their high wrongs I am struck to th'quick,
Yet, with my nobler reason 'gainst my fury
Do I take part. The rarer action is
In virtue, than in vengeance. They being penitent,
The sole drift of my purpose doth extend
Not a frown further. Go, release them, Ariel.
My charms I'll break, their senses I'll restore,
And they shall be themselves.

ARIEL I'll fetch them, sir. *Exit*

PROSPERO Ye elves of hills, brooks, standing lakes, and groves,
And ye that on the sands with printless foot
Do chase the ebbing Neptune, and do fly him
When he comes back; you demi-puppets, that
By moon-shine do the green sour ringlets make,
Whereof the ewe not bites; and you, whose pastime
Is to make midnight mushrooms, that rejoice
To hear the solemn curfew; by whose aid –
Weak masters though ye be – I have bedimmed
The noontide sun, called forth the mutinous winds,
And 'twixt the green sea and the azured vault
Set roaring war. To the dread rattling thunder
Have I given fire, and rifted Jove's stout oak
With his own bolt; the strong-based promontory
Have I made shake, and by the spurs plucked up
The pine and cedar; graves at my command
Have waked their sleepers, oped, and let 'em forth
By my so potent art. But this rough magic
I here abjure. And when I have required
Some heavenly music – which even now I do –
To work mine end upon their senses that
This airy charm is for, I'll break my staff,
Bury it certain fathoms in the earth,
And deeper than did ever plummet sound
I'll drown my book.

The court party enters. Prospero praises and weeps with Gonzalo, criticises Alonso and Sebastian, and though recognising Antonio's evil nature, forgives him. Prospero decides to dress as the Duke of Milan.

'There stand, / For you are spell-stopped.' Prospero now has all his enemies in his power within a magic circle.

1 Questions of staging (in small groups)

Act out the stage direction. For example, just how does Prospero trace out a circle on the stage? What is Alonso's 'frantic gesture'? How does Gonzalo 'attend' his king?

None of the court party can hear Prospero yet. His words are addressed to different groups or individuals (and sometimes to himself or to the audience). Work through lines 58–87, a short section at a time. Identify to whom Prospero speaks, his tone of voice, and where he pauses. Also consider the gestures he could make. For example, in one production, Prospero violently slapped Antonio's face before saying 'Flesh and blood' (line 74).

solemn air harmonious music (believed to cure madness)
sociable sympathetic
Fall fellowly drops weep friendly tears
mantle cover
loyal sir faithful courtier
Home fully
furtherer accomplice
reasonable shore shore of reason
discase me remove my magic cloak
sometime Milan formerly Duke of Milan

Solemn music. [Prospero traces out a circle on the stage.] Here enters ARIEL *before; then* ALONSO *with a frantic gesture, attended by* GONZALO; SEBASTIAN *and* ANTONIO *in like manner attended by* ADRIAN *and* FRANCISCO. *They all enter the circle which Prospero had made, and there stand charmed; which Prospero observing, speaks*

A solemn air, and the best comforter
To an unsettled fancy, cure thy brains,
Now useless, boiled within thy skull. There stand,
For you are spell-stopped.
Holy Gonzalo, honourable man,
Mine eyes, ev'n sociable to the show of thine,
Fall fellowly drops. The charm dissolves apace,
And as the morning steals upon the night,
Melting the darkness, so their rising senses
Begin to chase the ignorant fumes that mantle
Their clearer reason. O good Gonzalo –
My true preserver, and a loyal sir
To him thou follow'st – I will pay thy graces
Home both in word and deed. Most cruelly
Didst thou, Alonso, use me, and my daughter.
Thy brother was a furtherer in the act –
Th'art pinched for't now, Sebastian. Flesh and blood,
You, brother mine, that entertained ambition,
Expelled remorse and nature, who, with Sebastian –
Whose inward pinches therefore are most strong –
Would here have killed your king; I do forgive thee,
Unnatural though thou art. Their understanding
Begins to swell, and the approaching tide
Will shortly fill the reasonable shore
That now lies foul and muddy. Not one of them
That yet looks on me, or would know me. Ariel,
Fetch me the hat and rapier in my cell.

[*Exit Ariel*]

I will discase me, and myself present
As I was sometime Milan. Quickly, spirit,
Thou shalt ere long be free.

Ariel sings about a future of everlasting summer, and is sent by Prospero to fetch the sailors. Prospero presents himself to the amazed court. Alonso asks for Prospero's forgiveness, and resigns all claim to Milan.

---

1 Ariel's song (in pairs)

Ariel looks forward to a life without winter in which he will enjoy carefree summer. The traditional music for Ariel's song is quite easy to find, but try inventing your own to express Ariel's delight at the prospect of freedom.

2 'So, so, so'

Think about why Prospero says 'So, so, so' at line 96. The stage direction seems to suggest that he is commenting on the neatness of his costume as Duke of Milan. But what other possibilities are there? Is he reflecting on Ariel's freedom? Or is this the moment when he breaks his staff? Suggest other explanations which you think are likely.

3 'Behold'...

Prospero first becomes visible to the court party at line 106. Only one line before, Gonzalo has called for 'Some heavenly power' to guide the court party off the island which fills them with fear. If you were directing the play, what stage business would you use to clearly associate Prospero with that 'heavenly power'?

4 Alonso repents

Alonso is profoundly affected by the sight of Prospero. His madness ends, he resigns all claim to Milan, and he asks Prospero to pardon him.

Invent actions to accompany Alonso's lines 111–20. Then, before you turn the page, guess how Gonzalo, Antonio and Sebastian will react.

---

attire him dress Prospero
couch rest, sleep
presently immediately
drink the air before me fly incredibly swiftly
assurance certainty
thou beest you are
enchanted trifle magical trick
crave call for, demand

ARIEL [*returns with hat and rapier*], *sings, and helps to attire him*

ARIEL Where the bee sucks, there suck I;
In a cowslip's bell I lie;
There I couch when owls do cry;
On the bat's back I do fly,
After summer merrily.
Merrily, merrily, shall I live now,
Under the blossom that hangs on the bough.

PROSPERO Why that's my dainty Ariel. I shall miss thee,
But yet thou shalt have freedom. [*Arranging his attire*] So, so, so.
To the king's ship, invisible as thou art;
There shalt thou find the mariners asleep
Under the hatches. The master and the boatswain
Being awake, enforce them to this place;
And presently, I prithee.

ARIEL I drink the air before me, and return
Or ere your pulse twice beat. *Exit*

GONZALO All torment, trouble, wonder, and amazement
Inhabits here. Some heavenly power guide us
Out of this fearful country!

PROSPERO Behold, sir king,
The wrongèd Duke of Milan, Prospero.
For more assurance that a living prince
Does now speak to thee, I embrace thy body,
And to thee, and thy company, I bid
A hearty welcome.

[*He embraces Alonso*]

ALONSO Whether thou beest he or no,
Or some enchanted trifle to abuse me,
As late I have been, I not know. Thy pulse
Beats as of flesh and blood; and since I saw thee,
Th'affliction of my mind amends, with which
I fear a madness held me. This must crave,
And if this be at all, a most strange story.
Thy dukedom I resign, and do entreat
Thou pardon me my wrongs. But how should Prospero
Be living, and be here?

Prospero embraces Gonzalo. He reminds Antonio and Sebastian that he knows of their treachery to the king, but forgives Antonio. Alonso regrets the loss of his son. Prospero says he has recently lost his daughter.

---

1 Don't trust appearances

All the visitors to the island have had such extraordinary experiences that they are unwilling to trust their own eyes, 'Whether this be, / Or be not, I'll not swear' (lines 122–3). 'Subtleties' (line 124) were sugar-covered sweets served at the end of a banquet. They were made in the shape of mythical figures or buildings. Suggest why Prospero chooses to compare the courtiers' experiences to such sweets.

2 Genuine forgiveness? (in small groups)

One actor said:

> Prospero clearly says lines 130–2 between clenched teeth. He's forcing himself to forgive Antonio, and is not truly forgiving at all.

Talk together about whether you think Prospero's forgiveness of Antonio is full and sincere, or grudging and contemptuous.

How does Antonio respond to Prospero's forgiveness and to the demand to hand back the dukedom? Advise the actor.

3 Loss (in pairs)

Take parts as Alonso and Prospero and read aloud lines 134–52, emphasising the words 'lost', 'loss' and 'lose'. Perhaps Shakespeare was deliberately repeating the words to echo the Christian belief that loss is necessary in order to find God. Decide whether or not you think Shakespeare intended to express the idea that redemption and forgiveness can come only through suffering. Give reasons for your decision.

---

confined limited
subtleties deceptions, magical qualities
brace pair
justify proclaim
rankest worst
woe sorry
like loss similar loss
her sovereign aid the help of Patience
as late and as recent
dear grievous
means much weaker less to support me

PROSPERO [*To Gonzalo*] First, noble friend,
Let me embrace thine age, whose honour cannot
Be measured or confined.
[*Embraces Gonzalo*]
GONZALO Whether this be,
Or be not, I'll not swear.
PROSPERO You do yet taste
Some subtleties o'th'isle, that will not let you
Believe things certain. Welcome, my friends all.
[*Aside to Sebastian and Antonio*] But you, my brace of lords, were I so minded
I here could pluck his highness' frown upon you
And justify you traitors. At this time
I will tell no tales.
SEBASTIAN The devil speaks in him!
PROSPERO No.
For you, most wicked sir, whom to call brother
Would even infect my mouth, I do forgive
Thy rankest fault – all of them – and require
My dukedom of thee, which perforce I know
Thou must restore.
ALONSO If thou beest Prospero,
Give us particulars of thy preservation,
How thou hast met us here, whom three hours since
Were wracked upon this shore; where I have lost –
How sharp the point of this remembrance is –
My dear son Ferdinand.
PROSPERO I am woe for't, sir.
ALONSO Irreparable is the loss, and patience
Says it is past her cure.
PROSPERO I rather think
You have not sought her help, of whose soft grace
For the like loss, I have her sovereign aid,
And rest myself content.
ALONSO You the like loss?
PROSPERO As great to me, as late; and supportable
To make the dear loss have I means much weaker
Than you may call to comfort you; for I
Have lost my daughter.

Alonso wishes that Ferdinand and Miranda were married, and he was dead. Prospero comments on the courtiers' amazement, then reveals Ferdinand and Miranda playing chess. Ferdinand expresses gratitude to the sea.

'Sweet lord, you play me false.' In Shakespeare's theatre, Prospero probably drew a curtain at the back of the stage to reveal the lovers playing chess (then an aristocrats' game).

1 Arguing already?

How do you think Ferdinand has played Miranda false (line 172)? Has he cheated, or just made a clever chess move? Suggest why you think the lovers speak in this way.

mudded…bed buried in the mud of the sea-bed
admire wonder
devour their reason are open-mouthed in disbelief
do offices of truth work properly
natural breath merely air
chronicle story
relation tale
requite reward
discovers reveals
wrangle dispute
compass surround

ALONSO A daughter?
O heavens, that they were living both in Naples,
The king and queen there! That they were, I wish
Myself were mudded in that oozy bed
Where my son lies. When did you lose your daughter?

PROSPERO In this last tempest. I perceive these lords
At this encounter do so much admire
That they devour their reason, and scarce think
Their eyes do offices of truth, their words
Are natural breath. But howsoe'er you have
Been jostled from your senses, know for certain
That I am Prospero, and that very duke
Which was thrust forth of Milan, who most strangely
Upon this shore, where you were wracked, was landed
To be the lord on't. No more yet of this,
For 'tis a chronicle of day by day,
Not a relation for a breakfast, nor
Befitting this first meeting. Welcome, sir;
This cell's my court. Here have I few attendants,
And subjects none abroad. Pray you look in.
My dukedom since you have given me again,
I will requite you with as good a thing,
At least bring forth a wonder, to content ye
As much as me my dukedom.

Here Prospero discovers FERDINAND *and* MIRANDA, *playing at chess*

MIRANDA Sweet lord, you play me false.

FERDINAND No, my dearest love, I would not for the world.

MIRANDA Yes, for a score of kingdoms you should wrangle,
And I would call it fair play.

ALONSO If this prove
A vision of the island, one dear son
Shall I twice lose.

SEBASTIAN A most high miracle.

FERDINAND Though the seas threaten, they are merciful;
I've cursed them without cause.
[*He kneels before Alonso*]

ALONSO Now all the blessings
Of a glad father compass thee about.
Arise, and say how thou cam'st here.

Miranda marvels at the sight of the king and courtiers. Ferdinand tells his story, and Prospero urges that sorrows be forgotten. Gonzalo rejoices at the happy outcome of the voyage.

---

1 'O brave new world'

Miranda's wonder at the sight of so many strangers is charged with dramatic irony. The 'beauteous mankind' she sees includes usurpers and would-be murderers. Aldous Huxley's novel, *Brave New World*, uses Miranda's words ironically to describe a far from human future world.

Advise the actor playing Prospero how to speak his response (line 184) to Miranda's delighted exclamation. Think particularly about whether his tone of voice should be heavily ironic, or gentle and sympathetic.

2 'Lasting pillars'

Take Gonzalo literally! He enthusiastically recommends that the happy outcome should be recorded 'With gold on lasting pillars'. Such pillars could be marble columns, or the 'pillars of Hercules', which were the emblem of the Holy Roman Emperor.

Design your own version of Gonzalo's 'lasting pillars', including the inscription written on them (lines 206–13). Add illustrations to show each happy outcome.

3 Over-optimistic?

Gonzalo claims that each person has 'found' him- or herself as a result of the voyage and shipwreck (lines 206–13). But has each character really learned more about themself from their ordeal? Does each now possess increased self-knowledge and understanding?

Turn to the list of characters on page 1. Consider each character in turn and ask yourself if Gonzalo's claim is justified for that particular character.

---

eld'st acquaintance longest time
immortal providence divine fortune
renown glowing reports
heaviness sorrow
inly inwardly
chalked forth marked, signed
Was Milan thrust was Prospero banished
issue descendants
lasting pillars marble columns

MIRANDA O wonder!
How many goodly creatures are there here!
How beauteous mankind is! O brave new world
That has such people in't!

PROSPERO 'Tis new to thee.

ALONSO [*To Ferdinand*] What is this maid with whom thou wast at play?
Your eld'st acquaintance cannot be three hours.
Is she the goddess that hath severed us,
And brought us thus together?

FERDINAND Sir, she is mortal;
But by immortal providence, she's mine.
I chose her when I could not ask my father
For his advice, nor thought I had one. She
Is daughter to this famous Duke of Milan,
Of whom so often I have heard renown,
But never saw before; of whom I have
Received a second life; and second father
This lady makes him to me.

ALONSO I am hers.
But O, how oddly will it sound, that I
Must ask my child forgiveness!

PROSPERO There, sir, stop.
Let us not burden our remembrances with
A heaviness that's gone.

GONZALO I have inly wept,
Or should have spoke ere this. Look down, you gods,
And on this couple drop a blessèd crown;
For it is you that have chalked forth the way
Which brought us hither.

ALONSO I say 'amen', Gonzalo.

GONZALO Was Milan thrust from Milan, that his issue
Should become kings of Naples? O rejoice
Beyond a common joy, and set it down
With gold on lasting pillars: in one voyage
Did Claribel her husband find at Tunis,
And Ferdinand her brother found a wife
Where he himself was lost; Prospero, his dukedom
In a poor isle, and all of us ourselves,
When no man was his own.

Alonso blesses Ferdinand and Miranda. Gonzalo jokingly greets the Boatswain, who announces that the ship is as seaworthy as ever. Alonso is amazed by everything he sees and hears.

---

1 Anyone in mind?

Alonso condemns anyone who does not wish happiness for Ferdinand and Miranda, 'Let grief and sorrow still (always) embrace his heart'. Decide whether Alonso should look directly at Sebastian and Antonio as he speaks lines 214–15, giving reasons for your choice.

2 Echoes of the tempest

Gonzalo's friendly mocking of the Boatswain, 'Now, blasphemy…', echoes the opening scene of the play. Turn back to page 5 to remind yourself of what Gonzalo said about the Boatswain. Also decide whether or not you think the Boatswain really is a blasphemer (someone who speaks irreverently about God or religion). Gonzalo's memory may be playing him false.

3 The Boatswain's story (in small groups)

The story the Boatswain tells is full of striking detail (lines 230–40). Bring it to dramatic life by acting it out. One person reads the lines aloud, pausing after each short section (often a single word). In the pause, the others act out the story and provide sound effects.

Notice how Shakespeare makes the Master memorable. He only appeared in the first four lines of the play. Now he is described as 'Cap'ring to eye her' (dancing for joy at the sight of his undamaged ship).

---

swear'st grace overboard by swearing made God abandon our ship
glasses hours (see also line 186)
tight and yare shipshape and ready to sail
clapped under hatches imprisoned below deck
trim undamaged state
divided from them separated from the rest of the crew
moping in a daze
diligence hard worker
more than…conduct of something inexplicable
rectify correct

ALONSO [*To Ferdinand and Miranda*] Give me your hands:
Let grief and sorrow still embrace his heart
That doth not wish you joy.
GONZALO Be it so, amen.

Enter ARIEL, *with the* MASTER *and* BOATSWAIN *amazedly following*

O look, sir, look, sir, here is more of us!
I prophesied, if a gallows were on land
This fellow could not drown. [*To Boatswain*] Now, blasphemy,
That swear'st grace overboard – not an oath on shore?
Hast thou no mouth by land? What is the news?
BOATSWAIN The best news is, that we have safely found
Our king and company. The next, our ship,
Which but three glasses since we gave out split,
Is tight and yare and bravely rigged as when
We first put out to sea.
ARIEL [*To Prospero*] Sir, all this service
Have I done since I went.
PROSPERO [*To Ariel*] My tricksy spirit.
ALONSO These are not natural events, they strengthen
From strange, to stranger. Say, how came you hither?
BOATSWAIN If I did think, sir, I were well awake,
I'd strive to tell you. We were dead of sleep,
And – how we know not – all clapped under hatches,
Where, but even now, with strange and several noises
Of roaring, shrieking, howling, jingling chains,
And more diversity of sounds, all horrible,
We were awaked, straightway at liberty;
Where we, in all our trim, freshly beheld
Our royal, good, and gallant ship; our master
Cap'ring to eye her. On a trice, so please you,
Even in a dream, were we divided from them,
And were brought moping hither.
ARIEL [*To Prospero*] Was't well done?
PROSPERO [*To Ariel*] Bravely, my diligence. Thou shalt be free.
ALONSO This is as strange a maze as e'er men trod,
And there is in this business more than nature
Was ever conduct of. Some oracle
Must rectify our knowledge.

Prospero promises to explain. He sends Ariel to fetch Caliban, Stephano and Trinculo. They arrive. Caliban admires the courtiers. Prospero describes the drunkards and admits responsibility for Caliban.

'How fine my master is!' Caliban faces Prospero before the king and courtiers. But Antonio and Sebastian are cynical to the end, commenting on Caliban's market value.

1 'This thing of darkness, I / Acknowledge mine'

Many critics believe that, in lines 275–6, Prospero does much more than acknowledge that Caliban is his servant. They argue that Prospero accepts that he, too, has an evil side to his nature, and that his exile on the island has taught him that. Talk together about what you think of this interpretation. Ask each other such questions as: 'If Caliban is Prospero's evil nature, what is Ariel?' and 'In what tone does Prospero speak the line?'

beating on worrying about
picked leisure a chosen moment
shortly single soon and in private
Coragio courage
Setebos Caliban's and Sycorax's god
badges emblems on their clothes
make flows and ebbs cause the tides
And deal in her…power use the moon's power without her permission
demi-devil half-devil

PROSPERO Sir, my liege,
Do not infest your mind with beating on
The strangeness of this business. At picked leisure,
Which shall be shortly single, I'll resolve you,
Which to you shall seem probable, of every
These happened accidents. Till when, be cheerful
And think of each thing well. [*To Ariel*] Come hither, spirit,
Set Caliban and his companions free:
Untie the spell.

Exit Ariel

[*To Alonso*] How fares my gracious sir?
There are yet missing of your company
Some few odd lads that you remember not.

Enter ARIEL, *driving in* CALIBAN, STEPHANO *and* TRINCULO *in their stolen apparel*

STEPHANO Every man shift for all the rest, and let no man take care for himself; for all is but fortune. Coragio, bully-monster, coragio.

TRINCULO If these be true spies which I wear in my head, here's a goodly sight.

CALIBAN O Setebos, these be brave spirits indeed!
How fine my master is! I am afraid
He will chastise me.

SEBASTIAN Ha, ha!
What things are these, my lord Antonio?
Will money buy 'em?

ANTONIO Very like. One of them
Is a plain fish, and no doubt marketable.

PROSPERO Mark but the badges of these men, my lords,
Then say if they be true. This misshapen knave,
His mother was a witch, and one so strong
That could control the moon, make flows and ebbs,
And deal in her command, without her power.
These three have robbed me, and this demi-devil –
For he's a bastard one – had plotted with them
To take my life. Two of these fellows you
Must know and own; this thing of darkness, I
Acknowledge mine.

CALIBAN I shall be pinched to death.

Trinculo staggers about and Stephano has severe cramps. Ordered by Prospero to behave, Caliban hopes for wisdom and forgiveness. He rejects Stephano. Prospero invites Alonso and the others to hear his story.

---

1 Drunk or hung-over? (in pairs)

Both Trinculo and Stephano seem very much the worse for drink. In some productions, they are presented as suffering from severe hang-overs, rather than as being drunk. How would you direct them to behave in this final appearance?

Also decide how you would stage their exit. Do they hang their stolen clothes on the line? How do they behave towards each other? It can help if you take parts and, in role, tell your partner just what you think of him.

2 Caliban's last words

Lines 293–6 are Caliban's final words in the play. How accurately do they express his real feelings? Does he lie to Prospero when he promises to behave well and 'seek for grace'? Do you think he really has learned to be wise? Does he threaten or strike Stephano? Use your answers to these questions to work out how Caliban speaks the lines, and how he leaves the stage.

3 'Every third thought shall be my grave'

The play seems to be ending happily. Prospero looks forward to his departure for Naples, to the marriage of Ferdinand and Miranda, and to his return to Milan. But, like so much else in *The Tempest*, Prospero's line 310 is enigmatic. It could mean that he will be pre-occupied with death, or that his other thoughts will be of Miranda and Milan, or it might have some quite different meaning. Reflect on how you interpret Prospero's thoughts and feelings at this moment, and suggest how you think the line should be spoken.

---

reeling ripe legless, staggeringly drunk
gilded 'em made them so red-faced
fly-blowing decay (because I'm pickled, i.e. preserved)
trim it handsomely behave well
grace pardon, goodness
luggage stolen clothes
train followers
waste spend
accidents events, incidents
nuptial wedding, marriage

ALONSO Is not this Stephano, my drunken butler?
SEBASTIAN He is drunk now; where had he wine?
ALONSO And Trinculo is reeling ripe. Where should they
Find this grand liquor that hath gilded 'em?
[*To Trinculo*] How cam'st thou in this pickle?
TRINCULO I have been in such a pickle since I saw you last, that I fear me will never out of my bones. I shall not fear fly-blowing.
SEBASTIAN Why how now, Stephano?
STEPHANO O touch me not! I am not Stephano, but a cramp.
PROSPERO You'd be king o'the isle, sirrah?
STEPHANO I should have been a sore one then.
ALONSO [*Gesturing to Caliban*] This is as strange a thing as ere I looked on.
PROSPERO He is as disproportioned in his manners
As in his shape. Go, sirrah, to my cell;
Take with you your companions. As you look
To have my pardon, trim it handsomely.
CALIBAN Ay that I will; and I'll be wise hereafter,
And seek for grace. What a thrice-double ass
Was I to take this drunkard for a god
And worship this dull fool!
PROSPERO Go to, away.
ALONSO Hence, and bestow your luggage where you found it.
SEBASTIAN Or stole it rather.
[*Exeunt Caliban, Stephano and Trinculo*]
PROSPERO Sir, I invite your highness and your train
To my poor cell, where you shall take your rest
For this one night, which, part of it, I'll waste
With such discourse as I not doubt shall make it
Go quick away: the story of my life,
And the particular accidents gone by
Since I came to this isle. And in the morn
I'll bring you to your ship, and so to Naples,
Where I have hope to see the nuptial
Of these our dear-belovèd solemnised,
And thence retire me to my Milan, where
Every third thought shall be my grave.

Prospero promises a favourable voyage to Naples, and sets Ariel free. Alone on stage, Prospero admits that all his magical powers have gone. He asks the audience for applause, and for forgiveness to set him free.

1 *'Exeunt all'*: everyone leaves the stage

The way in which characters leave the stage can reflect how they think and feel at the end of the play. Work out your own suggestions for each character. Use the following points to help your thinking:

Ferdinand and Miranda Do they look forward to the future with total pleasure?

Antonio and Sebastian They have not acknowledged their wickedness, and have spoken no words of repentance. How do they behave?

Alonso, Gonzalo and the courtiers As king, does Alonso expect to leave first? Or has his experience made him humble?

Ariel Ariel says nothing when Prospero gives him his freedom. In one production, he spat in Prospero's face and scornfully left the stage. In one well-known outdoor production, he ran delightedly across the surface of a lake into the darkness.

2 Prospero's epilogue

Prospero now finds himself in the same position as Ariel and Caliban. He must plead to a superior power (the audience) for his freedom. It was a convention in many Elizabethan and Jacobean plays for an actor to step out of role at the end and ask the audience for applause. But Prospero seems to stay in role, hoping to be released from the island, so that he may journey to Naples.

Imagine that the actor playing Prospero asks you for advice: 'Should I step out of role, and show that I am only an actor, or should I stay in role as Prospero? Whichever I do, how should I perform the Epilogue, line by line?' Make your reply.

auspicious gales favourable breezes
expeditious speedy
charms magic powers
confined imprisoned
spell enchantment (by lack of applause)
bands bonds (imprisonment)
Gentle breath favourable comment
want lack
prayer the success of my plea (or the audience's prayers)
indulgence pardon, applause

ALONSO I long
To hear the story of your life; which must
Take the ear strangely.

PROSPERO I'll deliver all,
And promise you calm seas, auspicious gales,
And sail so expeditious that shall catch
Your royal fleet far off. My Ariel, chick,
That is thy charge. Then to the elements
Be free, and fare thou well. Please you draw near.

Exeunt all [*except Prospero*]

EPILOGUE, *spoken by* PROSPERO

Now my charms are all o'erthrown,
And what strength I have's mine own –
Which is most faint. Now 'tis true
I must be here confined by you,
Or sent to Naples, let me not,
Since I have my dukedom got
And pardoned the deceiver, dwell
In this bare island, by your spell;
But release me from my bands
With the help of your good hands.
Gentle breath of yours my sails
Must fill, or else my project fails,
Which was to please. Now I want
Spirits to enforce, art to enchant,
And my ending is despair,
Unless I be relieved by prayer
Which pierces so, that it assaults
Mercy itself, and frees all faults.
As you from crimes would pardoned be,
Let your indulgence set me free. *Exit*

Looking back at the play

Acitivities for groups or individuals

1 Final image

In one production, Ariel returned to the stage after Prospero's exit. He carried Prospero's staff, and clearly intended to take over the island and make slaves of Caliban and the spirits. Talk together about what you think of ending the play in this way. Suggest the final image the audience would see in your production. Who is left as master of the island?

2 Emotional journeys

Shakespeare frequently shows characters learning from the suffering they endure in the course of a play. In *The Tempest*, many characters undergo just such an 'emotional journey', and are changed as a result. Find a way of showing the 'emotional journey through the play' of three or four characters of your choice. Identify what they have learned. Who do you think changes the most?

3 Mirror images?

The play contains many parallel incidents or qualities. For example, there are conspiracies against sleeping victims; similar usurpation plots; Ferdinand and Caliban are both forced to carry logs, and so on. Decide whether or not you think that Ariel and Caliban are similarly linked.

4 Last glimpse of the island

Choose a character. Imagine him or her looking back at the island from the ship which is now heading towards Naples. Write the thoughts which go through his or her mind as the island slowly fades from view.

5 'Desert Island Discs' (in pairs)

In the radio programme 'Desert Island Discs', a famous person is invited to imagine that they have been shipwrecked on a desert island. They choose their eight favourite pieces of music, and are interviewed on their life-story. They are also invited to answer questions about which book and which luxury item they would choose to have with them on the island. Take parts as an interviewer and a character from *The Tempest*, and conduct your own radio interview.

6 Observing the unities

A well-known theory of drama (based on the writings of the ancient Greek philosopher Aristotle) states that, if a play is to possess aesthetic harmony, it must observe the unities of action, time and place. This means it should have a single action lasting less than twenty-four hours, enacted in a single location. *The Tempest* is unlike all of Shakespeare's other plays, with the exception of *The Comedy of Errors*, in that it observes the unities:

> *Time* The action of the play takes place in under four hours (see Act 1 Scene 2, lines 239–41, and Act 5 Scene 1, lines 186 and 223).
> *Place* Apart from Scene 1, everything takes place on the island.
> *Action* All the sub-plots link neatly to the central plot of the usurpation of Prospero and his plan to regain his dukedom.

Draw a 'Time line' to represent 2 p.m. to 6 p.m., and place the various events in the play on it, from the shipwreck to the final scene.

7 Press conference (in large groups)

On the return to Naples, a press conference is arranged. All the characters will be closely questioned by press, radio and television reporters. Take parts and stage the press conference. Some characters, such as Prospero and Alonso, may have prepared a speech in advance to deliver at the quayside.

8 Ranking the characters

Draw a line about twenty centimetres long. Label one end 'youngest' and the other end 'oldest'. Place each character somewhere on the line, according to their age. Then try the same activity using different labels at each end of the line, for example:

> 'most loved by Prospero' ____________ 'most hated by Prospero'
> 'most evil' ____________________________________ 'most moral'
> 'character I like the most' _________ 'character I dislike the most'
> 'part I'd most like to play' ___________ 'part I'd least like to play'

Compare your ordering of characters with that of other students, and talk together about the reasons for any differences. Make up other ways of ranking the characters, for example, 'high social status' and 'low social status'.

What is *The Tempest* about?

Imagine that you can travel back in time to around 1611. You meet William Shakespeare a few minutes after he has finished writing *The Tempest*, just before he takes it into rehearsal with his company, The King's Men. You ask him, 'What is the play about?'

Perhaps Shakespeare would reply, 'Think about the title, *The Tempest*. You can take it quite literally, as the story of a group of people who are shipwrecked in a great storm. Alternatively, you can take it symbolically, as representative of the mental and emotional turmoil suffered by nearly all the characters. You can read it on many different levels.'

But nobody can really know how Shakespeare would reply. Like all great artists, Shakespeare does not seem interested in explaining his work, but leaves it up to others. He just says, 'Here it is. Read it, perform it, make of it what you will.' There has been no shortage of responses to that invitation! Hundreds of answers to the question 'What is *The Tempest* about?' have been offered since it was first performed. The following pages give some of those different readings. They show that the play can be interpreted in many ways, all of which have a claim to being true.

First, you could think of *The Tempest* simply as a story. Before the play begins, Prospero, Duke of Milan, has been overthrown by his brother Antonio, aided by King Alonso of Naples and the king's brother, Sebastian. Prospero and his daughter, Miranda, have been exiled to an island, where, over a period of twelve years, he has perfected his magic and made Caliban his slave. In the play, Prospero causes his enemies to be shipwrecked on the island, and subjects them to different ordeals arranged by his servant, the spirit Ariel. Finally, Prospero forgives his enemies, but only Alonso is fully repentant. The play ends with Prospero regaining his dukedom, and with the prospect of the marriage of Alonso's son, Ferdinand, to Miranda. Ariel is set free, and Prospero and the others prepare to return home.

Or you could think of *The Tempest* as a particular type of play, such as a 'romance'. *The Tempest* is the last in a group of four plays (often called 'the late plays') which Shakespeare wrote at the end of his career. The others are *Pericles*, *Cymbeline* and *The Winter's Tale*. They are romances or tragic-comedies, containing elements of both tragedy and comedy, but ending happily. Romance plots contained all kinds of fairy-tale improbabilities and fantasies. They mixed together love, magic, storms, feasts, miracles and journeys to faraway places, where magical events occurred. Romance stories often told of loss and recovery, of royal children thought to be dead, but, like Ferdinand, found to be living.

The Tempest has also been interpreted as a masque. It may be Shakespeare's response to the courtly masque, a type of the theatre which developed, and was very popular, during the reign of King James I (see pages 108 and 110). Such entertainments contained spectacular theatrical effects, music, dance, and bizarre and mythological characters. King James and his court would have expected a masque to end in the triumph of virtue, peace and beauty, with harmony restored under a rightful monarch.

Another view of *The Tempest* is to see it as a play with a particular purpose. Many people think that Shakespeare had a specific purpose in mind when he wrote *The Tempest*, but the suggested purposes are very different! Some see it as Shakespeare writing about himself as Prospero, bidding farewell to his art as a playwright. Others claim that the play was written to celebrate the marriage of Princess Elizabeth, daughter of King James I. Other people interpret the play as a record of Shakespeare's spiritual progress; a history of Elizabethan/Jacobean theatre; a comment on politics in seventeenth-century Europe; a study of Renaissance science; or a criticism of colonialism. However, it is very unlikely that Shakespeare had a single purpose in mind. Like all his plays, *The Tempest* gives everyone plenty of opportunity to exercise their imagination!

One way of answering the question 'What is *The Tempest* about?', is to identify the themes of the play. These include:

Usurpation (the overthrow of a rightful ruler)
The play contains rebellions, political treachery, mutinies and conspiracies. All kinds of challenges to authority are made:

- The Boatswain orders the king and courtiers off the deck
- Antonio seizes the dukedom of Milan from his brother, Prospero
- Caliban tries to rape Miranda
- Antonio and Sebastian plot to kill Alonso and Gonzalo
- Caliban, Stephano and Trinculo plot to kill Prospero.

Nature versus nurture (natural growth versus education and civilisation)
Two major views of nature are explored in the play. The first is that

nature, left alone, grows to perfection. Gonzalo's 'commonwealth' speech (Act 2 Scene 1, lines 142–58) expresses this view, namely a belief in the inherent goodness of a natural society which grows to harmony and happiness, without social engineering of any sort.

The second view is that nature is inherently bad, and therefore cannot be left to its own devices, but must be controlled and educated in order to become good. In this second view, nurture (civilisation, education, art) is superior to nature. This belief is expressed in Prospero's opinion of Caliban 'on whose nature nurture can never stick'. Here, nature is inherently untrustworthy, savage and evil: Caliban is incapable of being educated or trained.

Imprisonment and freedom

All the characters in the play suffer some kind of confinement:

- Prospero and Miranda are exiled to the island
- Caliban is enslaved first by Prospero, then by Stephano
- Ariel, imprisoned by Sycorax, must also serve Prospero, and is threatened with harsh punishment
- Ferdinand is forced to carry logs as Prospero's prisoner
- Alonso, Sebastian and Antonio are driven into madness
- Stephano, Trinculo and Caliban are tormented by Prospero's spirits
- the sailors are confined, fast asleep, below decks.

Everyone yearns for freedom, but in very different ways. Caliban's idea of liberty is to exchange one master for another. Gonzalo dreams of a Utopian republic in which people are free of every possible constraint. Prospero's final action is to set Ariel free, and his last words in the play ask the audience to 'set me free'.

Forgiveness and reconciliation

For much of the play, it is not clear exactly what Prospero intends to do to his enemies. Is his desire for revenge, or for reconciliation? The appearance of Iris in the masque may be a symbol that Prospero intends mercy. Iris is goddess of the rainbow, and the rainbow is a sign that a storm has ended and a new start can be made. Like the other 'late plays' (see page 148), *The Tempest* ends in forgiveness and reconciliation after great suffering. Prospero relents, and decides that forgiveness is the better guide to human conduct, 'The rarer action is in virtue, than in vengeance' (Act 5 Scene 1, lines 27–8). Revenge gives way to forgiveness and pardon.

Illusion and magic

Things are not what they seem in *The Tempest*. The play begins with an illusion: the shipwreck is an act of Prospero's magic. What seems so disastrously real, is only a fiction. Most of the characters in the play cannot trust the evidence of their eyes. The supernatural powers which Prospero draws upon, and the legacy of Sycorax, make the island a bewildering, baffling place.

Colonialism

The story of an expedition to colonise part of America may well have inspired Shakespeare to write *The Tempest* (see pages 152–7). The travellers' tales of the 'New World' brought back to England by explorers and colonisers, are strongly echoed in the play. Many of the colonists were fired by the prospect of unlimited wealth and a life of ease. In their greed, the colonists viewed the native peoples as little more than beasts, fit only to be slaves. There are sombre echoes of this viewpoint in the portrayal of Caliban, who is subjected to slavery first by Prospero, then by Stephano.

Sleep and dreams

Sleep and dreams recur throughout the play. Prospero sends Miranda to sleep, Ariel causes Alonso and Gonzalo to sleep, thus provoking murderous thoughts in Antonio and Sebastian. The sailors are asleep under hatches for almost the entire play. Caliban's dreams are so wonderful that he longs to sleep again. Gonzalo's vision of his 'commonwealth' is a dream of what the perfect, Utopian society might be like. The spectacular banquet and masque also have dream-like qualities.

Change and transformation (metamorphosis)

The turbulence of the storm which begins the play changes into the apparent peace and harmony of the ending. The masque suggests the changing seasons of nature: springtime and harvest. Similarly, many of the characters experience a sea-change: Alonso's despair turns to joy; Prospero's wish for vengeance metamorphoses into forgiveness; and Caliban's evil intentions become a desire for grace.

Imagine that you are asked to explain what *The Tempest* is about by a six-year-old child, by a student of your own age, and by your teacher or lecturer. Speak or write your reply to each, using pages 148–51 to help you.

A real-life tempest

In writing *The Tempest*, Shakespeare was probably influenced by a true story which was the talk of all London in 1610. In May 1609, a fleet of nine ships set out from England. Five hundred colonists were on board. Their goal was the newly-founded colony of Virginia, where the settlers intended to begin a new life. They hoped for fabulous fortunes because of everything they had heard about the natural riches of America. But disaster struck.

In the great storm, the flagship the *Sea-Adventure*, carrying the expedition's leader, Sir Thomas Gates, became separated from the fleet. The ship was driven onto the rocks of Bermuda, a place feared by sailors and known at the time as the Devil's Islands ('The still-vexed Bermudas' of Act 1 Scene 2, line 229). The rest of the fleet sailed on, reached Virginia, and sent back news to London of the loss of the expedition's leader with all of his one hundred and fifty companions.

For almost a year, England mourned. Then, in late summer of 1610, astonishing news arrived. The lost colonists had miraculously survived and reached Virginia! Apparently, the *Sea-Adventure* had run aground close to shore. All the passengers and crew had escaped safely, and were able to salvage most of the supplies from the ship. They discovered that Bermuda was far from being the desolate and barren place of legend. It had fresh water, and a plentiful supply of food in fish, wild pigs, birds and turtles. The survivors set about building two boats so that they could sail on to Virginia.

It seemed as if providence smiled. But human nature soured the good fortune of the survivors, and mutiny broke out. There were attempts to seize the stores. Malicious rumours spread, and a bid was made to murder the governor and take over the island. Only after great difficulties did Sir Thomas Gates and his companions set sail for Virginia. Even then, two mutineers elected to stay behind on Bermuda.

Shakespeare probably found the inspiration for *The Tempest* in the pamphlets, written in 1610–11, which described the misadventures of the would-be colonists. The following extracts from the original pamphlets suggest how Shakespeare's dramatic imagination was stirred by this miraculous tale of loss and rediscovery, of the benevolence of nature, and of mutinies against an island's leader.

On St James' day, a TERRIBLE TEMPEST overtook them, which scattered the whole fleet ... his ship, torn or lost in the TEMPEST.

Ariel's story (Act 1 Scene 2, lines 195–206)

An apparition of a little round light, like a faint star, trembling and streaming along with a sparkling blaze half the height upon the mainmast, and shooting sometime from shroud to shroud ... and for three or four hours together, or rather more, half the night it kept with us, running sometimes along the mainyard and then returning.

The abundance of the island

The richest, pleasantest, and most healthful place we had ever seen ... The shore and bays round about when we landed first afforded great store of fish ... Fowl that is in great store, small birds, sparrows fat and plump like a bunting, ... White and grey hernshaws (herons), bitterns, teal, snipes, crows, and hawks ... cormorants, bald coots, moorhens, owls and bats, in great store ... A kind of web-footed fowl there is, of the bigness of an English green plover, or sea-mew.

The rebellion against Prospero

Yet was there a worse practice, faction and conjuration afoot, deadly and bloody, in which the life of our governor, with many others, were threatened.

Discontented rebels made a greater shipwreck by the tempest of dissension; every man over-valuing his own worth would be a commander, every man underprizing another's value denied to be commanded.

a Imagine that you are one of the survivors of the wrecked *Sea-Adventure*. You return to London, and are something of a celebrity because of your miraculous escape. Mr William Shakespeare invites you to visit him in order to talk over a play he has in mind, inspired by your adventure. Role-play the meeting with a partner, then write up the conversation.

b Imagine that you are one of the two mutineers who chose to stay behind on the island of Bermuda. Tell your story, including the reasons why you joined the expedition in the first place.

c National newspapers did not exist in Shakespeare's time, so news was often spread by pamphlets. You have been asked to write such a pamphlet, based on the accounts of some of the returned colonists.

Colonialism and *The Tempest*

A 1970 production of *The Tempest* presented the play as a story of colonial exploitation. The director, Dr Jonathan Miller, described it as 'the tragic and inevitable disintegration of more primitive culture as the result of European invasion and colonisation'. He compared Stephano and Trinculo to foreign soldiers, who patronise or bully the native population: 'they shout loudly at the people to make them understand, make them drunk and get drunk themselves'. Caliban was 'the demoralised, detribalised, dispossessed, suffering field-hand'.

Miller's interpretation was in sharp contrast to the traditional image of Prospero as a benevolent ruler. However, there is no doubt that the history of the colonisation of the Americas was a story of horror and savagery. Although some Europeans tried to uphold the principle of benign civilisation, the overwhelming evidence is that of brutal conquest.

The colonists from the Old World (Europe) found their beliefs and culture challenged by their experience of what they called the New World (North and South America). Increasingly throughout the twentieth century, interpretations and productions of *The Tempest* have stressed the contrasts and conflicts between Prospero and Caliban, between colonist and native inhabitant.

Economic exploitation

The Europeans sought to profit through trade, exploiting the rich resources of the New World. But did they have the right to take possession, by gun and sword, of the land which the native Indians saw as theirs? Resentful of Prospero's take-over, Caliban claims, 'This island's mine', to which Prospero replies, 'Thou most lying slave'. Trinculo wonders how much money he could get for exhibiting Caliban at an English fair. Similarly, Sebastian and Antonio comment on Caliban's market value (Act 5 Scene 1, lines 264–6). European greed was a driving force of so-called 'civilisation'.

Social class

The notion of social hierarchy was firmly fixed in the European mind. Most people believed it to be God-given. At the top was the king, who claimed to rule by divine right. Below him were aristocrats and courtiers, and so on, down to the lowest peasant. The 'masterless man', (a person without a superior), was (and still is) seen as a terrible threat to social order. The European colonists of the New World brought back reports that the natives lived without a rigid social hierarchy, each man the equal of others. To Prospero, Caliban represents potential anarchy, and must therefore be controlled by harsh punishment.

Sexuality

Travellers' tales reported that the marriage customs of Europe were quite unknown in the Americas. In the colonists' eyes, debauchery and vice flourished without control among the natives. To the Europeans, such free love was abhorrent. In this European view, Caliban's attempted rape of Miranda is evidence of his fundamentally evil nature, justifying constraint and harsh punishment. From the same viewpoint, Prospero's strict control of the sexual relations of Miranda and Ferdinand expresses a higher state of civilisation, characterised by restraint, abstinence and self-discipline.

Religion

A major aim of colonisation was to spread the Christian gospel. The native Americans were seen as 'heathen', worshipping false and savage gods. Colonisation was, in part, a religious crusade sanctioned by divine right. However harsh the settlers' treatment of the natives, it was often justified by the claim that the intention was to save their souls, and bring them to the true religion. Caliban is described as a son of the Devil and a witch (Act 5 Scene 1, lines 268–73). He worships the Patagonian god Setebos.

Race

European Christians believed in their ethnic superiority over the native races of the New World. Such people were seen as 'savages' or cannibals ('Caliban' is almost an anagram of 'cannibal'). They were seen as treacherous by nature, repaying kindness with treachery. Even the colour of their skin was held to be a mark of their less-than-human status, 'this thing of darkness', as Prospero describes Caliban (Act 5 Scene 1, line 275). Many colonists thought that such people could legitimately be treated as useful slaves ('He does make our fire, / Fetch in our wood', Act 1 Scene 2, lines 312–13).

Language

Throughout history, conquerors and governments have tried to suppress or eliminate the language of certain groups, defining it as 'inferior'. Within living memory, Welsh children were forbidden to speak their native language in school. The ancient Greeks called anyone who did not speak Greek a 'barbarian' (speaking 'baa-baa' language). The word itself is onomatopoeic, like 'double-Dutch' or 'mumbo-jumbo' and suggests what the Greeks saw as 'nonsense' language.

In Shakespeare's time, most Europeans believed that only their own languages were civilised. Overseas languages were 'gabble', without real meaning. Caliban must be taught to speak properly in order to know his own meaning. The mark of savagery was not knowing English or Spanish or some other European language. Caliban expresses the resentment of the enslaved, 'You taught me language, and my profit on't is, I know how to curse'.

The Europeans set about what they believed to be their divinely ordained task of taking ownership of the New World. They felt confident that they were educating the uneducated, bringing spiritual enlightenment to the heathen, and extending the domains of their European monarchs. Hand in glove with these aims went the profitable exploitation of what was seen as a wilderness, neglected by its native inhabitants. But it must have looked very different through the eyes of the native inhabitants. They saw their freedom vanish as their lands were seized, and their old religions destroyed. Millions found themselves forced into virtual slavery.

Some critics accuse Shakespeare of giving a Eurocentric view of colonisation in *The Tempest*. They argue that the story is told only from Prospero's point of view. Caliban has little chance to tell his side of the story of harsh subjugation, of how the master/slave relationship quickly replaced that of teacher/pupil. However, Shakespeare also gives voice to a quite different view of the New World in the play. Gonzalo's description of the commonwealth (Act 2 Scene 1, lines 142–58) is that of an ideal world, a benign Utopia of peace and harmony.

a Who has most right to claim ownership of the island? Work with a partner, and take parts as Caliban and Prospero. Argue your case that the island belongs to *you*.

b Do you think that Shakespeare's *The Tempest* is a justification of colonialism, a criticism of it, or that it does not express any point of view on colonisation?

c Write the word 'civilisation' in the centre of a large sheet of paper. Spend five to ten minutes brainstorming everything that comes into your mind when you think of civilisation. Write down each thought on the paper. Afterwards, study everything you have written to see if you can arrive at a definition of 'civilisation'.

A 1586 engraving of Europeans being greeted on arrival in Virginia. Like Caliban, the native inhabitants often revealed the natural resources of their lands to the newcomers. Think about how the picture can help your understanding of *The Tempest*, and find one or two lines from the play to make a suitable caption.

Magic in *The Tempest*

The play is full of magic and its effects. The opening tempest which seems so real is only an enchantment. Music is everywhere. Strange shapes, fantastic creatures and wonderful illusions appear. Ariel's song expresses the mysterious transformations which take place, as everything undergoes 'a sea-change, into something rich and strange'.

In Shakespeare's England, the line between magic and science was not clearly drawn. Many people believed in witches, or in magicians like the legendary Dr Faustus, who sold his soul to the Devil in exchange for magical powers. When Shakespeare created Prospero, he may have had in mind Dr John Dee, a famous Elizabethan mathematician and geographer. Some of Dr Dee's work was genuinely scientific, but he was widely regarded as a '*magus*', someone who dabbled in magic. A *magus* could be an alchemist (an early scientist who attempted to change base metals into gold), or an astrologer and sorcerer, who communicated with the occult or spirit world.

Prospero can be seen as a *magus*. He has devoted his life to secret studies in order to gain magical powers, his 'art'. Prospero's supernatural powers are astonishing. He has control over earth, air, fire and water. He can raise and calm tempests, command his spirits to produce fantastic banquets and masques, make himself invisible, and control Caliban with cramps and pinches. He can call up music, and send people to sleep. When he decides to renounce his magical powers, Prospero recalls all the miracles he can perform: dimming the sun, commanding the winds, making storms at sea, splitting oaks with lightning bolts, and causing earthquakes. He can even raise the dead from their graves.

The play contrasts Prospero's benign magic with the evil magic of Sycorax, Caliban's mother, and her god, Setebos. Prospero's charms and spells are aimed at achieving virtue and goodness: 'there's no harm done', he assures Miranda when she grieves for the shipwrecked crew and passengers. Sycorax's sorcery is devilish, and Shakespeare adds reminders of Caliban's wicked ancestry ('got by the devil himself').

But Prospero's magic powers are limited, and he depends on luck to help him. For example, it was 'providence divine' which brought him safely to the island, and 'bountiful Fortune' and 'a most auspicious star' which brought his enemies within his reach. Although Prospero can control the natural world, he can only hope that human nature will change. He cannot make Ferdinand and Miranda fall in love, only bring them together and hope that they will do so. He cannot cause his enemies to experience remorse and repentance for their deeds. His magic seems unable to cause Sebastian or Antonio to undergo a change of heart for their misdeeds.

Prospero's books, Royal Shakespeare Company, 1993. The signs of Prospero's powers are his magic garment, his staff, and above all, his books ('that I prize above my dukedom'). Caliban identifies the source of Prospero's powers very precisely: 'possess his books; for without them he's but a sot, as I am…Burn but his books' (Act 3 Scene 2, lines 85–9).

a Just what were the books that Prospero brought with him from Milan, and from which he acquired his magic powers? Make up a list of titles for the books in Prospero's library. Choose one book and design it, showing the cover illustration, binding, contents page, and how each page would be written and illustrated.

b Find quotations or examples in the play to illustrate Prospero's magical powers, as described in the third paragraph on page 158.

c Identify one act of magic from each of the five acts. Present a mime or dance drama of *The Tempest* based only on those five moments.

Ariel, Caliban and Prospero

Ariel

Ariel is described in the list of characters as 'an airy spirit', and has been played by both male and female actors. Ariel appears in different guises: a flaming light in the storm, a nymph of the sea, a harpy at the banquet, Ceres in the masque. At Prospero's command, Ariel performs near-impossible feats, such as fetching 'dew from the still-vexed Bermudas', treading 'the ooze of the salt deep' and running 'upon the sharp wind of the north'.

Imprisoned by Sycorax for refusing to obey her orders, and freed by Prospero's magic, Ariel yearns for freedom throughout the play. Prospero's attitude to his spirit-servant is ambiguous. Sometimes he seems affectionate, calling Ariel 'bird', 'chick', 'my fine spirit'. But, at other times, he calls Ariel 'moody' or 'malignant thing'. When Ariel demands 'my liberty', Prospero threatens him with twelve more years of imprisonment.

Ariel's language often expresses rapid movement and breathless excitement. There is a childlike eagerness to please in 'What shall I do? Say what? What shall I do?'. It is Ariel who teaches Prospero forgiveness and pity. Describing the plight of Prospero's enemies, Ariel says that the sight of them would make Prospero feel compassion (Act 5 Scene 1, lines 18–20):

ARIEL ...if you now beheld them, your affections
Would become tender.
PROSPERO Dost thou think so, spirit?
ARIEL Mine would, sir, were I human.
PROSPERO And mine shall.

Some critics see Ariel as representing Prospero's imagination, or as the personification of imagination. Other critics see him as Prospero's chief informer and secret policeman. What is your view of Ariel? Think about the following:

- Male or female or...? (The stage directions refer to 'him'.)

- Does Ariel serve Prospero with eager and spontaneous willingness, or with reluctance and bad temper?
- Does Ariel love Prospero, or fear and detest him, or feel other emotions?
- What are Prospero's feelings for Ariel: genuine love, or a harsh master's demand to have his every wish instantly performed?
- How does Ariel compare with Puck in *A Midsummer Night's Dream*?

A poster advertising a 1904 production. Design your own poster with Ariel as the main subject.

Caliban

Caliban is probably about twenty-four years old at the start of the play. He is described as a 'savage and deformed slave' in the list of characters, and in all kinds of uncomplimentary ways in the play, for example, 'filth', 'hag-seed', 'misshapen knave' and 'monster'. On stage, he has been played as a lizard, a dog, a monkey, a snake and a fish. He was once played as a tortoise, and was turned over onto his back by Prospero when he became unruly.

In the eighteenth century, the comic aspects of the role were emphasised. Caliban was a figure of fun, not to be taken seriously. In recent times, performances have emphasised Caliban's human and tragic qualities, not just his wickedness. He has increasingly been seen as a native dispossessed of his language and land by a colonial exploiter (see pages 154–7). To help you form your own view of Caliban, think about each of the following:

Victim? A ruthless exploiter takes over Caliban's island, forcing him into slavery. He is seen by the shipwrecked Europeans as an opportunity to make money.

Savage? Caliban is brutish and evil by nature, incapable of being educated or civilised ('on whose nature nurture can never stick'). His plot against Prospero reflects his violent and vindictive nature.

Servant? Caliban deserves to be a slave. He merely exchanges a harsh master (Prospero), for a drunken one (Stephano), and wants to serve as a 'foot-licker'.

Contrast? Caliban's function in the play is to act as a contrast to other characters. For example, lust versus true love (Ferdinand), natural malevolence versus civilised evil (Antonio).

Noble savage? Until Prospero arrived, Caliban lived in natural freedom. He loves the island, and his language eloquently expresses some of the most haunting poetry in the play when he responds to Ariel's music: 'the isle is full of noises'.

Symbol of wickedness? Shakespeare's contemporaries wrongly believed that deformity was a sign of the wickedness of parents. Prospero claims that Caliban is the son of a witch and the Devil.

Does Caliban remain on the island after everyone else leaves for Naples? Or does he also go to Naples, and then on to Milan with Prospero? Consider each possibility in turn, then write an account of what happens to Caliban after the end of the play.

Make a list of all the names Caliban is called by Stephano and Trinculo ('fish', 'shallow monster', 'howling monster', and so on). What does the list suggest to you about both Caliban and the two shipwrecked Europeans?

Recognisable human being or stereotype of a savage and deformed slave? Compare the way in which Caliban was presented in this 1951 production with other pictures on pages 30, 68, 86, 120 and 140. Then decide how you would portray Caliban on stage.

Prospero

Prospero was traditionally portrayed as a well-intentioned magician, a serene old man whose 'project' was to restore harmony and achieve reconciliation. But, in many twentieth-century productions, he has been played as a much more ambiguous figure, harsh and demanding, impatient and deeply troubled. Opinions about him vary widely.

Name Prospero is Latin for 'I cause to succeed, make happy and fortunate'. Bearing this definition in mind, how appropriate do you think Prospero's name is?

Magus and scholar Prospero successfully learns to practise magic. His books and his spirits enable him to control the natural world, but to what extent can he control human nature – his own and others'?

Prince Prospero's self-centred pursuit of study made him neglect his civic duties, and subsequently led to his overthrow. When he is reinstated as Duke of Milan, will he devote himself single-mindedly to good government ('Every third thought shall be my grave')?

Father Is Prospero a loving, kind and devoted father to Miranda? Or is he bad-tempered, dictatorial and irritable?

Revenger Prospero pardons his enemies at the end of the play, but was his original plan to seek revenge for his overthrow and banishment?

Man At the end of the play, Prospero admits to his weakness as a fallible human being: 'Now my charms are all o'erthrown, / And what strength I have's mine own'. What has he learned in the course of the play?

Master Prospero controls Caliban harshly with cramps and pinches, and has not got a good word to say about him. Is he a colonialist exploiter, or a benevolent ruler of the island?

Actor-manager Prospero is like a theatre director. He stages the opening tempest; he ensures that Gonzalo and Alonso sleep, so provoking a murder attempt; he is the unseen observer of his daughter and his enemies; and he produces the banquet and the masque. Are all the other characters merely his 'actors'?

Shakespeare Some people believe that Shakespeare wrote the part of Prospero as a self-portrait, particularly in his farewell to his 'art' at Act 5 Scene 1, lines 33–57. Do you?

Prospero as *magus*.

Compare the way in which Prospero is presented here with the illustrations on pages 8, 22, 30, 38, 128, 140 and 159. Then suggest how he would appear in your production.

The language of *The Tempest*

The Tempest is Shakespeare's second shortest play – only *The Comedy of Errors* is shorter. The language chosen by Shakespeare contributes to the brevity of the play. It is compressed and dense, often in irregular rhythm or word order, and with different verb tenses sometimes used in the same sentence. Occasionally, words are omitted, increasing the sense of urgency or anger.

1 The language of nature

The play abounds in language which evokes the rich variety of the natural world: sea, air, earth and wildlife. Almost every page contains some aspect of nature:

> 'barren ground – long heath, brown furze', 'dew', 'wind', 'frost', 'fresh-brook mussels, withered roots, and husks', 'pig-nuts…jay's nest…clust'ring filberts…Young scamels', 'Toothed briars, sharp furzes, pricking gorse, and thorns'.

Turn, at random, to any page of the script. List every word on it which refers to nature. Repeat with six to eight other pages. Present your 'nature words' as a display which illustrates the natural world of the play. For example, you could decide to contrast the threatening and the benign aspects of nature.

2 The language of master and slave

Prospero and Caliban only appear together in Act 1 Scene 2, and Act 5 Scene 1. Remind yourself of everything Prospero says to Caliban, and classify each sentence or phrase as either 'orders', 'threats and curses', or 'other language'. What do you find? Repeat the activity with the language which Caliban which speaks directly to Prospero.

3 Songs and music

The Tempest contains more music than any of Shakespeare's other plays. It has nine songs (pages 33, 61, 67, 75, 93, 111 and 131). Work through the play listing each time music is played or songs are sung. Suggest what you think is the dramatic purpose or effect of each one. Alternatively, choose one song and work out an appropriate way in which to perform it.

4 Repetition

Pages 149–51 indicate the way in which the themes and actions of *The Tempest* mirror each other (for example, usurpation, freedom and imprisonment, dreams and sleep). Shakespeare uses similar repetition in the language of the play. Sometimes words or phrases are repeated ('We split, we split!', 'Twelve years since, Miranda, twelve years since'). Often the echoes are in sounds, an effect known as 'alliteration'. Prospero's language in Act 1 Scene 2 is full of such repetition of words and sounds. For example, in lines 32–3, not only are words repeated ('which thou'), but there are also repetitions of letters: the 's' in 'saw'st sink. Sit', and the 'n' sound in 'now know'.

Turn to pages 9–41 and find further such examples of repetition in Prospero's language. Then look for examples elsewhere in the play. Talk together about what effect you think they have when the language is read or heard. For example, many people claim that repetition has a hypnotic, rhythmical effect, which is both pleasing to the ear, and seductively persuasive.

5 Dramatic irony

Dramatic irony occurs when the audience knows something that a character on stage does not. It can arise from language, for instance when Miranda exclaims 'How beauteous mankind is! O brave new world' at the sight of a group which includes the villainous Antonio and Sebastian. Or it can arise from the contrasts in a scene, such as the harmony of the masque being followed by the sight of three bedraggled drunkards. Identify two or three other examples of dramatic irony in the play.

6 A soliloquy for Prospero?

Prospero's language rarely gives direct access to his thoughts. He tells stories, gives orders, comments on the action, and renounces his magic in long, spell-like speeches. At the end of the play, he speaks directly to the audience. Yet, unlike many of Shakespeare's other major characters, such as Hamlet or Iago, he does not have a soliloquy in which he reveals what is really on his mind. For example, although he speaks about his 'project' (plan), he never says whether his original aim in raising the tempest was to exact revenge, or whether he planned, from the outset, to forgive his enemies.

Think about possible reasons why Shakespeare did not give Prospero such a soliloquy. Then try your hand at writing a soliloquy for Prospero, in which he reveals his most private thoughts.

7 Creating images with the hyphen

In this play of improbable happenings, Shakespeare frequently uses the hyphen to create compound words which conjure up vivid images. He puts words together to present new challenges to the imagination. For example, in Act 1 the compound words include: 'blue-eyed', 'brine-pits', 'fresh-brook', 'hag-born', 'hag-seed', 'o'er-prized', 'over-topping', 'sea-change', 'sea-nymphs', 'sea-sorrow', 'sea-storm', 'side-stitches', 'sight-outrunning', 'still-vexed', 'up-staring', 'wide-chopped'.

Some compound words are easy to understand or imagine, like 'sea-swallowed' and 'pinch-spotted'. Others are vividly powerful, but cannot be pinned down to a single, exact meaning, such as 'sight-outrunning'. Shakespeare may have used these hyphenated words because their instability expresses the sense of wonder and ever-changing reality which runs through the play.

Create your own compound words. Prospero calls Caliban 'hag-seed', seed (child) of a witch. Make up a few hyphenated words of your own to describe Prospero or other characters of your choice.

8 Lost words

The meaning of unfamiliar words can often be understood from their context, although some words in the play have disappeared from use today. For example, in Act 2 Scene 2: 'bombard', 'butt of sack', 'doit', 'flats', 'inch-meal', 'mow', 'neat's leather', 'poor-John', 'siege', 'trenchering', 'troth', 'urchin-shows', 'young scamels'. A suggested meaning of each unfamiliar word is given throughout this edition.

Just what are the 'young scamels' which Caliban promises to bring to Stephano (Act 2 Scene 2, line 158)? 'Scamels' may be seagulls or clams, or may have meant something quite different in Shakespeare's time. Today, no one really knows. The word reflects the nature of *The Tempest* itself: enigmatic, not able to be tied down to a single meaning, and therefore very imaginative!

Exploring unfamiliar meanings can be a fascinating activity. It involves searching in a good dictionary for the origins of the words, and to see how they have changed over the years. Take one scene and write down all the words which are unfamiliar to you. Find out their meanings and decide, giving your reasons, whether there are any that you would change in performance to make them understandable to a modern audience.

9 Threats and curses

Antonio and Sebastian curse the Boatswain in Act 1 Scene 1. Prospero and Caliban rage at each other in Act 1 Scene 2. Collect up some of the threats and curses from the play, share them between you, and hurl them at each other.

10 The language of the theatre

Shakespeare's interest in the theatre is evident throughout *The Tempest*. There are spectacular dramatic events, such as the shipwreck, the banquet and the masque. The language is full of echoes of acting and plays. Ariel is like a stage-manager as he 'performs' the tempest, and arranges the banquet and the masque. When he seizes control in Milan, Antonio is like an actor, who would 'have no screen between this part he played / And him he played it for'. Later, as he plots Alonso's murder, Antonio uses the language of the theatre: 'cast...perform...act...prologue... discharge' (Act 2 Scene 1, lines 243–6). Prospero reflects on the way in which life itself is like a stage pageant, whose actors and theatre ('the great globe itself') vanish into thin air (Act 4 Scene 1, lines 147–58). In one production, Prospero was played as an actor-manager, emphasising the theatrical aspects of the story. Suggest how you would stage the play with Prospero as actor-manager.

11 'The isle is full of noises'

Take the cue offered by Caliban in Act 3 Scene 2, line 130, and create a sound-track of sound effects for the play.

12 The sea

Images of the sea occur frequently throughout the play ('sea-sorrow', 'sea-change', 'sea-swallowed', 'never-surfeited sea', 'still-closing waters', 'sea-marge'). Immediately after the shipwreck, Miranda's first words describe 'the wild waters', and tell of the sea dashing out the lightning (Act 1 Scene 2, lines 1–5). Prospero speaks of the tempest which he and Miranda endured when they were exiled from Milan, 'th'sea, that roared to us'. At the end of the play, Ferdinand says, 'Though the seas threaten, they are merciful'.

Use the 'sea words' in the paragraph above to prepare a talk for the director to give to a cast of actors about to begin rehearsals for a production of *The Tempest*.

Staging *The Tempest*

Shakespeare probably wrote *The Tempest* around 1610–11. Only two performances of the play are known for certain to have taken place during his lifetime, both at the court of King James I. *The Tempest* has always been extremely popular on stage, but for over two hundred years it was not as Shakespeare originally wrote it!

In 1667, the play was rewritten as *The Enchanted Island*. Only one-third of Shakespeare's play was included, and a great deal was added. Caliban and Miranda were given sisters. A male character appeared, Hippolito, Duke of Mantua. He had never seen a woman, and would be under a curse if he *did* see one. The masque and the role of Sebastian were left out entirely, although much more comedy, dance and music was inserted. Expensive stage machinery created spectacular effects, particularly in the storm scene, and in the flying of Ariel and the other spirits.

This version of *The Tempest* was revived in many adaptations during the eighteenth and nineteenth centuries, with every production aiming at enthralling theatrical spectacle. One version shifted the storm scene to the start of Act 2, so that late-comers to the theatre would not miss the elaborate stage effects. Another version contained thirty-two songs.

These operatic and balletic versions of *The Tempest* attracted large audiences, but were often criticised for being more like pantomimes. In 1815, one famous critic, William Hazlitt, was outraged by what he saw, calling it, 'travesty, caricature...vulgar and ridiculous...clap-trap sentiments...heavy tinsel'. He was tempted never to see another Shakespeare play!

In spite of all the criticism, the spectacular version of *The Tempest* was always popular with audiences. Each new production was hugely successful, and very profitable. It was not until the mid-nineteenth century that serious attempts were made to present the play as Shakespeare had written it.

Today, most stage productions of *The Tempest* make only minor changes to Shakespeare's script, and try to avoid the sentimental escapism of earlier versions. Instead, they take the opportunities that Shakespeare provides to explore the many ambiguities and conflicts which exist in the script. Even in these modern versions, special attention is paid to the opportunities for dramatic spectacle.

The Tempest has always been a source of inspiration for other artists, too. Mozart planned an opera based on it, but died before he could make his plan into music. Many novelists have written 'island stories', for example Daniel Defoe's *Robinson Crusoe*, William Golding's *Lord of the Flies* and Marina Warner's *Indigo*. Poets have been especially attracted by the play. Shelley, T. S. Eliot and W. H. Auden drew on *The Tempest*, and in the poem, 'Caliban upon Setebos', Robert Browning made Caliban extremely eloquent and intelligent. Aldous Huxley's novel *Brave New World* imagines a horrific future society, in which people are little more than robots. Screen and stage adaptations include *Forbidden Planet*, a Hollywood science-fiction film, and *Return to the Forbidden Planet*, a 1980s rock musical.

The stage set, Royal Shakespeare Company, 1982. Try your hand at designing a set for your own production.

William Shakespeare 1564–1616

1564 Born Stratford-upon-Avon, eldest son of John and Mary Shakespeare.
1582 Marries Anne Hathaway of Shottery, near Stratford.
1583 Daughter, Susanna, born.
1585 Twins, son and daughter, Hamnet and Judith, born.
1592 First mention of Shakespeare in London. Robert Greene, another playwright, described Shakespeare as 'an upstart crow beautified with our feathers…'. Greene seems to have been jealous of Shakespeare. He mocked Shakespeare's name, calling him 'the only Shake-scene in a country' (presumably because Shakespeare was writing successful plays).
1595 A shareholder in 'The Lord Chamberlain's Men', an acting company that became extremely popular.
1596 Son Hamnet dies, aged eleven.
Father, John, granted arms (acknowledged as a gentleman).
1597 Bought New Place, the grandest house in Stratford.
1598 Acted in Ben Jonson's *Every Man in His Humour*.
1599 Globe Theatre opens on Bankside. Performances in the open air.
1601 Father, John, dies.
1603 James I grants Shakespeare's company a royal patent: 'The Lord Chamberlain's Men' became 'The King's Men' and played about twelve performances each year at court.
1607 Daughter, Susanna, marries Dr John Hall.
1608 Mother, Mary, dies.
1609 'The King's Men' begin performing indoors at Blackfriars Theatre.
1610 Probably returned from London to live in Stratford.
1616 Daughter, Judith, marries Thomas Quiney.
Died. Buried in Holy Trinity Church, Stratford-upon-Avon.

The plays and poems
(no one knows exactly when he wrote each play)

1589–1595 *The Two Gentlemen of Verona, The Taming of the Shrew, First, Second and Third Parts of King Henry VI, Titus Andronicus, King Richard III, The Comedy of Errors, Love's Labour's Lost, A Midsummer Night's Dream, Romeo and Juliet, King Richard II* (and the long poems *Venus and Adonis* and *The Rape of Lucrece)*.
1596–1599 *King John, The Merchant of Venice, First and Second Parts of King Henry IV, The Merry Wives of Windsor, Much Ado About Nothing, King Henry V, Julius Caesar* (and probably the *Sonnets*).
1600–1605 *As You Like It, Hamlet, Twelfth Night, Troilus and Cressida, Measure for Measure, Othello, All's Well That Ends Well, Timon of Athens, King Lear.*
1606–1611 *Macbeth, Antony and Cleopatra, Pericles, Coriolanus, The Winter's Tale, Cymbeline, The Tempest.*
1613 *King Henry VIII, The Two Noble Kinsmen* (both probably with John Fletcher).
1623 Shakespeare's plays published as a collection (now called the First Folio).